JN302960

国際人になるための
Insight Track
モーゼの十戒に学べ

東京大学薬友会会長
小林 利彦 著 *Toshihiko Kobayashi*

【英訳文付】

JMP 日本医療企画

発刊に寄せて

東京大学・北海道大学名誉教授
（公財）微生物化学研究所所長
柴﨑正勝

　私が最も尊敬する先輩、小林利彦博士の著書『国際人になるためのInsight Track』の推薦文を書かせていただく事は、大変光栄であります。

　小林博士との最初の出会いは、昭和45年頃ではなかったでしょうか。大学紛争が一段落し、大学の研究室（当時の東京大学薬学部薬品製造化学教室）も落ち着きを取り戻し、研究に集中できる環境が整ったときです。小林博士がオーストラリア国立大学で博士号を取得され、三菱油化に入社されるまでの期間、共通の恩師の山田俊一先生が主催されておられた薬品製造化学教室へ研究生としてやってこられたのです。私は大学院修士課程の院生でした。当時の研究室は今では想像できない程の古典的なものでした。夏目漱石の"坊ちゃん"に出てくる東京大学の研究室を想像していただければよいでしょう。その頃の私は自分の研究に手一杯で、オーストラリアを始めとする海外での研究生活等にはあまり感心はありませんでした。

　そのようなわけで小林博士と数多くの議論をした記憶はありません。ただうすいブルーのコットンパンツをはいて黙々と研究をされている小林博士が強く記憶に残っております。この時代、小林博士と最もインパクトのあった出来事は、私が人生初の研究論文を英国化学会誌に投稿する時の経緯だと思います。恥ずかしながら私は論文を書くにあたって英

国際人になるための
Insight Track

―― モーゼの十戒に学べ

小林利彦 著

Recommendation

Masakatsu Shibasaki Ph.D.

Prof. Emeritus of University of Tokyo and HokkaidoUniversity Representative Director of Institute of Microbial Chemitry (IMC).

I am greatly honored to write this for a most respected senior Dr. Kobayashi's book, 'Insight Track – To Become an Internationally-Minded Person'.

I believe that I first met Dr. Kobayashi during the 1970. This was a period after the turmoil of the university's student movement, and academic activities were returning to normality. Also within the research laboratory of Department of Medicinal Chemistry and Process Chemistry , the environment had settled down, restoring an atmosphere which allowed faculty and students alike to focus upon research. It was within this period, that Dr. Kobayashi upon receiving his doctorate from the Australian National University, and prior to joining Mitsubishi Petrochemical had arrived as a postgraduate to the Research Department directed and overseen by our mutual mentor Professor Shunichi Yamada. At the time, I was studying for my master's degree. Compared to the research environment of today, it would be difficult to imagine, and explain the old fashioned atmosphere. Perhaps if you could picture the description of the University of Tokyo's research laboratory, out of the novel 'Botchan' by Soseki Natsume. In all honesty, at the time I was completely tied-up with my own research and had no real interest in with either Australian or for that matter overseas research activities.

It is for perhaps this reason, that I really do not have memories of numerous debates with Dr. Kobayashi. What I do strongly recall is Dr. Kobayashi figure, sporting light blue cotton slacks, persistently conducting research. During this period, the strongest impact I received from Dr. Kobayashi was

語らしい表現が全くできませんでした。実験をやっている小林博士にいろいろ尋ねながら、なんとか論文を執筆する事ができました。その原稿を山田教授にお見せしたところ、英語がうまいねと褒められました。原稿の英語はかなりの部分、小林博士によるものでしたが、その事を私は教授には報告しませんでした。意図的に報告しなかったのではなく、タイミングが合わなかったと言った方が正しいと思いますが。

　小林博士が企業へ入られた後は、私もハーバード大学に移り、それ程強い交流はなかったのですが、日本アップジョン社社長に就任されてから、現在に至るまで兄と弟のような関係が続いております。小林博士が社長兼米国本社副社長に就任された時、私も北海道大学薬学部の教授になっていました。会社の研究コンサルタントをしてほしいという事で、年に数回筑波の研究所を訪ね、研究指導をするかたわら、外資系企業の文化等々様々な知識を教えていただく事ができました。

　当時の最も強烈な記憶は、英語の達人と思っていた小林博士の社長車の中に英語の辞書が置いてあった事です。それと米国のアップジョン社との会議(毎週木曜日、夜9時から深夜2時)のために、米国調の素晴らしい社長室に布団が用意されていた事です。その後、やはり外資系企業リリー社の重役を務められ、その後は米国研究製薬工業協会の日本技術代表と、全ての仕事が国際人たる感覚がなければなし得ない人生を歩んでおられます。私が東京大学薬学部長の時、同窓会組織、薬友会の会長に就任していただき、現在に至っております。

　小林博士の人生哲学を通して私がいつも心がけている事は、起こってしまった事はくよくよ気にしない、常に前を向いて対処する姿勢です。さらには、自分が欲する事は積極的に狙いにいかなかったら絶対に手に

events leading up to when I was faced for the first time in my life with an opportunity to contribute an article to The Journal of Chemical Society (JCS ,British). To my embarrassment, writing the article in English is totally beyond me. While asking numerous questions to Dr. Kobayashi who was conducting his research, I was able to finish the article. Showing the completed article text to my mentor, Professor Yamada, I was praised for the good English. Although the majority of the English text was from Dr. Kobayashi, I neglected to mention this to Professor Yamada. Not doing so was not a purposeful act, but it was due to the timing, which was just not right was the true light of events.

After Dr. Kobayashi joined a business world , I relocated to Harvard University. Although we did not sustain a steady interaction, from when he was appointed president of Upjohn Japan, to today, we continue to enjoy an older brother, younger brother relationship. When Dr. Kobayashi was appointed president in Japan and vice president of U.S. Headquarters, I had become a professor at the University of Hokkaido. I was approached by Dr. Kobayashi to become a research consultant for the firm; through visiting the Tsukuba Research Laboratories several times a year, giving research guidance, I was continuing my professional research, and this opportunity provided many lessons and insight into the cultural aspects of a multinational corporation.

As expected, I had regarded Dr. Kobayashi as an English expert. What really surprised me at this time was when I discovered an English dictionary in his company assigned car. Added to this, for conference calls with U.S. Upjohn (every Thursday, from 9PM to 2AM), there was a Japanese futon mattress in his beautiful western style office. Following his tenure with Upjohn, Dr. Kobayashi became an executive at yet another U.S. firm, Eli Lilly, which was followed by his position as Japan Technical Representative of the Pharmaceutical Research and Manufacturers of America(PhRMA), which could only be achieved through truly understanding what it was to become an international minded individual. When I became the Pharmaceutical Sciences

する事はできない等の考えでしょうか。

　本書の中には国際人小林利彦博士の生き様、人生哲学が凝縮されています。ぜひ真剣に読んでいただけたらと心から希望する次第です。

Department Director of the University of Tokyo, Dr. Kobayashi became our alumni association 's chair to present.

Through Dr. Kobayashi's philosophy, I constantly keep in mind not to ponder on events of the past, but to always face forward to address anything that may come my way. Also, if there is a goal or objective that you wish to achieve, it must be pursued aggressively, or it will not become reality.

Within this book, you will discover the thoughts, lifestyle and philosophy of Dr. Toshihiko Kobayashi. I not only sincerely hope, but would strongly encourage readers to seriously take in its contents.

発刊に寄せて

ロンドン大学名誉教授
C. ロビン・ガネリン

　国際純正応用化学連合（IUPAC）医薬化学の活動を通じて20年余にわたり知己である小林利彦（Toshi）氏が、著者となる本書の紹介をすることは、大変な喜びです。

　1990年頃、IUPAC加盟国の学生に提供している医薬化学のトレーニングが、医薬産業における創薬に役立っているかという課題を二人で検討することになりました。Toshiが日本で検討を行い、二人の共同報告書をIUPAC誌に発表しました。それ以来、親密な交友を続け、現在もIUPACの医薬化学・創薬委員会でともに活動しています。

　Toshiは強力な国際的展望をもち、1974年にIUPACに関わって以来、多くの個人的な絆を維持しています。若い日に、オーストラリア国立大学の大学院であるジョーン・カーテイン医学研究所のA・アルバート教授(医化学)の門を叩いたことは、非常に賢明であったと思います。当時、教授は医薬化学の先駆者であり、今や医薬化学の偉大な学者として歴史に名を残しています。

　このような背景とともに、医薬産業界での強力かつ輝かしい経歴と、堪能な英語によるコミュニケーションにより、Toshiは、日米の強力な橋渡し役を担ってきました。三菱油化薬品株式会社（取締役、1984年）、

Recommendation

Charon Robin Ganellin Ph.D.
Prof. Emeritus of University College London

It is a pleasure to write an introduction for this work by Toshi Kobayashi who I have known for some 20 years through our many contacts over medicinal chemistry matters in the International Union of Pure and Applied Chemistry (IUPAC).

In the 1990's we had a close collaboration on the subject of whether the medicinal chemistry training received by students in various countries fitted them for research work in the pharmaceutical industry. Toshi investigated this for Japan and we had joint publications on the topic. We have kept in touch ever since, now in IUPAC's Subcommittee on Medicinal Chemistry and Drug Development.

Toshi has a strong international outlook and has made many personal contacts during his 40 years in pharmaceuticals and IUPAC, which he joined in 1974. Very early in his career (in 1970) he opted to study for a PhD in medical chemistry and very wisely chose to do this with Professor Adrian Albert at the John Curtin School of Medical Research, in the Australian National University, Canberrra. Albert, in his day, was one of the world's leading medicinal chemists, and now stands out in history as one of the past medicinal greats.

This background provided Toshi Kobayashi with the basis for a strong and distinguished career in the pharmaceutical industry and encouraged him to speak and communicate in the English language. Starting in Mitsubishi Yuka Pharmaceutical Co, where he reached the board, he then became part of the USA-Japan interface, firstly as President of Upjohn Pharmaceuticals (Ja-

アップジョン・ファルマスーテイカル株式会社社長、日本イーライリリー株式会社エクゼクテイブＶＰ、米国研究製薬工業協会（W—DC）対日技術代表として活動をしてきましたが、未だ米国シリコンバレーのバイオベンチャーのコンサルタントとして活躍しています。

　Toshiも余裕のある生活を考えていた矢先、順子夫人を循環器アタックで亡くしました。Toshi夫妻と、スコットランドのエジンバラの魚料理レストランで一緒に食事を楽しんだことは、懐かしい思い出です。

　Toshiの過去の経歴と国際的知名度を考えると、Toshi以外に本書『国際人になるためのInsight Track』を著すにふさわしい人物はいません。

pan), then as Executive Vice President of Eli Lilly (Japan), and finally as technical representative for Japan on the Pharmaceutical Research and Manufacturers of America organisation (PhRMA).

Toshi was never a passive member of the foregoing organisations. In IUPAC he became one of the founders of the Asian Federation of Medicinal Chemistry. From his PhRMA activities he helped to introduce metrics into the review process of the Pharmaceuticals and Medical Devices Agency (PMDA) in Japan. Toshi is still active and is consulting to help Silicon-Valley Bioventures.

Although Toshi might have looked forward to a pleasant retirement he has sadly lost his wife, Junko, who passed away last year due to cardiac events. Indeed, I recall the pleasure of meeting her with Toshi at a pleasant dinner in a fish restaurant in Edinburgh, Scotland, whilst attending an IUPAC meeting some years ago.

Considering Toshi's past career and his international outlook, he is just the right person to write a book: Insight Track comprising forty one (41) essays in a monthly journal

まえがき

　"An independent thinker（物真似でなく自身で考える）"。1967年から3年間、オーストラリア国立大学(ANU)のジョン・カーティン医学研究大学院の指導教官、W.L.F.アルマレゴ博士に叩き込まれた言葉である。これを基本理念に、1970年、夢を現実にする"まなびの道"に飛び込むことになった。1980年代、自分にとっての"天とは何か"を知る機会に恵まれた。自分の周りの方々が、自分にはないものを持っている貴重な先生であることを思い知ったのである。これを機に、人のお世話をすることが苦にならなくなり、最近は"情けは人のためならず"の結果をよく体験させてもらっている。同じく1980年代にはもう1つ"素心"という言葉を教わり、事にあたって動じないバランス感覚を持てるようになった。

　以上のような思考の回り道を歩みながらも、1970年に飛び込んだ世界は欧米中心の仕事であった。米国企業のエグゼクティブ、アカデミア関係にはイスラエル系の方が多い。なぜか私はこの方々の引き回しを受ける機会が多かった──米国人の同僚が羨むほどに。この先達の背景は何なのか──その文化的背景を少しずつ学ぶことにした。その様な環境で私自身が体験したことを語ることで、皆様が自らを律するため、また相手を洞察する力を研くためにお役に立てればと思い、㈱日本医療企画の好意により、私の体験を出版することになった次第である。

2014年5月吉日　　　　　　　　　　　　　　　　　　　　　　　小林 利彦

Forward (Introduction)

Toshihiko Kobayashi

"An independent thinker", over a period of three years from 1967, this phrase, or practice was drilled into me by my medical research postgraduate studies Counselor Professor W.L.F Armarego of The John Curtin School of Medical Research, Australian National University (ANU). Embracing this as my fundamental principles, in 1970 to realize my dream, I embraced the "path of learning". During the 1980s, I was blessed with an opportunity to learn "what is heaven" for me.

I was able to realize that I was surrounded by individuals who possessed what I lacked, thus I became to see them as valuable teachers. From this period, to provide assistance or helping others was no longer an anxiety, and recently I have experienced, as the old Japanese proverb says; "Charity is a good investment". It was also in the 1980s, in which I learned of the concept of sustaining unswerving determination with a sense of balance, reflected in the phrase, 'So- Shin'.

With the aforementioned principles, while taking a roundabout path; in 1970 I found that my career environment was western-centric. I discovered that many executives of American corporations, and academia related individuals share an Israeli background. I have no idea why, but I found that I was taken under the wing of these individuals to the envy of my colleagues. What was the influence of these senior individuals – it was to gradually absorb and increased awareness of their cultural background. It is through sharing the wisdom I received from these individuals, as well as my personal experiences within this specific environment that I hope will assist readers to personally establish discipline as well as hone their skills of observation and insight. I thank Nihon Iryo Kikaku for their graciousness in making it possible for my experiences to be published.

目次

発刊に寄せて：柴﨑正勝／C.ロビン・ガネリン ……………… 2
まえがき ……………………………………………………………… 12

第1章 国際人になるための十戒 …………… 19

第1話	文化の背景 ……………………………………………	20
第2話	グローバリゼーション──国境を越えて …………	26
第3話	日本、"Executive Pipeline"を ………………………	32
第4話	自らの天命を自覚せよ ………………………………	38
第5話	リーダー、「透明な頑固さ」を持て …………………	44
第6話	リーダー、自らを偶像化してはならない …………	50
第7話	自らの言葉を甘く見るな──言葉は消えない、実在する	56
第8話	素心──ものの本質を見極める心 …………………	62
第9話	An independent thinker ……………………………	68
第10話	「余人をもって代えがたい」はない ………………	74
第11話	敬愛するも従属せず …………………………………	80
第12話	人(他人・部下)を故意に殺めてはいけない ………	86
第13話	不倫はするな──責任を持てないなら不倫はするな	92
第14話	有形・無形を問わず、盗人になってはならない …	98
第15話	ウソをついてはいけない ……………………………	104
第16話	隣の芝生は青くない──羨望を断ち切れ …………	110
第17話	足るを知る人は心豊かなり …………………………	116
第18話	家族間でお金の貸し借りをしてはならない──十戒余話1	122
第19話	眞の愛と憎しみとは──十戒余話2 ………………	128
第20話	ブレンド化された民──十戒余話3 ………………	134
第21話	ゲノム解析──十戒余話4 …………………………	140

Contents

Recommendation : Masakatsu Shibasaki Ph.D. / Charon Robin Ganellin Ph.D. . . . 3
Forward (Introduction) 13

Chapter 1.
Ten Commandments in Becoming an Internationally 19

The First Narrative Cultural Background 21
The Second Narrative Globalization beyond National Borders 27
The Third Narrative Japan Inc. Strengthening the "Executive Pipeline" 33
The Fourth Narrative The Mission—God's will. 39
The Fifth Narrative A Leader's Fundamental Necessity, Clear Determination
  Filled with Confidence 45
The Sixth Narrative Leader, No Self-Idolization 51
The Seventh Narrative Beware of What You Say, Words Do Not Disappear 57
The Eighth Narrative Possess the Ability to Identify the True Nature of
  Any Given Thing 63
The Ninth Narrative An Independent Thinker 69
The Tenth Narrative Anyone is Expendable 75
The Eleventh Narrative To Honor but Not to Obey 81
The Twelfth Narrative Do Not Deliberately Kill 87
The Thirteenth Narrative Don't Commit Adultery If You Cannot Take the
  Responsibility 93
The Fourteenth Narrative Innocent or Guilty, Do Not Become a Thief 99
The Fifteenth Narrative Don't Lie 105
The Sixteenth Narrative The Other Man's Grass May Not Be Greener,
  Sever Thoughts of Envy 111
The Seventeenth Narrative Learn To Be Contended 117
The Eighteenth Narrative The Ten Commandments and Other Allegories (Part 1)
  Neither Lends or Barrows Among Family 123
The Nineteenth Narrative The Ten Commandments and Other Allegories (Part 2)
  True Love and Hate 129
The Twentieth Narrative The Ten Commandments and Other Allegories (Part 3)
  Blended Community 135
The Twentiet-First Narrative The Ten Commandments and Other Allegories (Part 4)
  Genetic Analysis 141

第2章 国際人になるための Insight Track ……… 147

- 第1話　目で話す人、耳で話す人、口で話す人——相手のタイプを見極めよ .. 148
- 第2話　天とは何か …………………………………………………… 154
- 第3話　誠心誠意——モスクワの友人A.グルシコフ氏 …………… 160
- 第4話　「思いついたらすぐやる」は両刃の剣 ……………………… 166
- 第5話　強い使命感を持て …………………………………………… 172
- 第6話　コンプライアンス遵守の徹底 ……………………………… 178
- 第7話　「エンパシー」の心を身につけよ …………………………… 184
- 第8話　どう違う——見ると相る …………………………………… 190
- 第9話　近いうちに——定量的か定性的か ………………………… 196
- 第10話　「遠交近攻」——ボスとの付き合いにどう生かす ………… 202
- 第11話　チームの協力体制づくり …………………………………… 208
- 第12話　キャリア女性のキューピッド——魂の通い合うパートナーを探せ … 214
- 第13話　女性エグゼクティブが時代を変える ……………………… 218
- 第14話　コーポレートガバナンス
　　　　　——スウェーデン・ビジネスモデルとバイキング ……… 224
- 第15話　名もなき道を行くなかれ …………………………………… 230
- 第16話　瞑想は経営の術なりや ……………………………………… 236
- 第17話　脈々と続く同族会社に学ぶ1——真のカスタマーは誰ですか ……… 242
- 第18話　脈々と続く同族会社に学ぶ2——創業者の信念の凄さ …… 248
- 第19話　忘れ得ぬ国際人1——柴﨑正勝氏と「サンデー・サイレンス」 …… 254
- 第20話　忘れ得ぬ国際人2——C.ロビン・ガネリン氏の「ヒスタミン・ロマンス」…. 260

あとがき ………………………………………………………………… 266

Chapter 2.
Insight Track —To Become an Internationally-Minded Person..147

Number One A Person Who Communicates with Their Eyes, a Person Who Communicates with Their Ears, and a Person Who Communicates with Their Mouth 149
Number Two What is Heaven? 155
Number Three Sincerity, A Friend in Moscow, Dr. Alexander Glushkof 161
Number Four Act Immediately on Inspirations—Double-Edged Sward 167
Number Five Possess a Sense of Mission 173
Number Six Loyalty to Compliance 179
Number Seven Possess "Empathy" 185
Number Eight The Difference between Seeing and Viewing 191
Number Nine 'In the Near Future', is This Quantitative or Qualitative? 197
Number Ten 'Interact with Those Who are Distant, Antagonize Those Who are Near'—How to Utilize This When Interacting the Boss 203
Number Eleven Building a Team Cooperation Structure—Listening To Opponents . 209
Number Twelve A Career Woman's Cupid 215
Number Thirteen Executive Women Change Generation 219
Number Fourteenth Corporate Governance—Swedish Business Model and Vikings ..225
Number Fifteenth Don't Take a Road with No Name 231
Number Sixteenth Importance of Mediation in Management 237
Number Seventeenth The Survival Capability of Family Controlled Companies (Part 1) —Who are Your Customers 243
Number Eighteenth The Survival Capability of Family Controlled Companies (Part 2) —Relentless Belief of Founders 249
Number Nineteenth Unforgettable International Person(1) —Prof. Masakatsu Shibasaki and Sunday Silence 255
Number Twentieth Unforgettable International Person(2) —Prof. Robin Ganellin and Histamine Romance 261

Acknowledgements 267

本書は、国際商業出版株式会社『国際医薬品情報』に2011年1月～2012年6月に連載された
「グローバリゼーション　国際人になるための十戒」(全21話)、および2012年7月～2014
年1月に連載された「グローバリゼーション　国際人になるためのInsightTrack」(全20話)を
初出とし、今回の出版に際して加筆・修正を加えております。

第1章
国際人になるための十戒

Chapter 1.
Ten Commandments
in Becoming an Internationally

第1話
文化の背景

　欧米の文化に対する私の学生時代の知識は、誰もが知っている程度のものだった。1967年、オーストラリア国立大学大学院に留学中、英国からの同僚とシェイクスピアについて語り、話が有名な喜劇「ヴェニスの商人」へ及ぶと、彼は「そんな話は知らない」と言って、さっさと実験室へ行ってしまった。後になって知ることになるが、シェイクスピアはこの戯曲によって、ユダヤの人々についての誤った印象を世間に広めてしまったのである。

　当時"チェコの春"が弾圧されて、チェコからの大学院生は帰国してしまい、また新聞紙上では北アイルランドとアイルランドの一神教同士の凄まじい戦いが報道されていた。これらを目の当たりにして、国際的視野を持った人を目指すならば、その国の文化が成り立っている背景についてもよく学ばねばならない、ということを知らされた。

　1976年にはこんな出来事もあった。研究契約をしていた米国製薬大手（現在でも世界ランク7位）のCEO、エグゼクティブVP、R&D担当VPと、三菱系石油化学会社の黒川久社長、大畑哲郎専務、藤井茂常務、それに私（当時課長）の会食が東京の有名フレンチ・レストランであった。デザートに及んだ時、エグゼクティブVPが「トシ、デザートは何がいいの？」と私に尋ねた。「日本のマスクメロンがいいと思いますよ」

The First Narrative
Cultural Background

When I was a student, my knowledge and understanding of the western culture was what can be referred to as an average, or 'what everyone else knew' level. In 1967 while studying at the Australian National University Graduate School, I became acquainted with a fellow student from England. While in the laboratory, we started to have a friendly conversation. The dialogue went into the realm of Shakespeare, however, when eventually it touched upon the famous 'The Merchant of Venice', my conversation partner stated "I don't know that story." Although it was later that I was to learn, that through this particular Shakespeare play, a warped, mistaken image of the Jewish people was globally established.

This was the period of the 'Prague Spring', in which political suppression was taking place in Czechoslovakia. In the midst of Czech students returning to their homeland, and seeing newspapers filled with reports on the ferocious conflict between North Ireland and Ireland, both sides' believers of a monotheistic religion, I perceived that those who strive to attain an international perspective, must initially make an effort to study and understand any given country's cultural background.

In 1976 I was involved in a particular event that reinforced this concept. It was at a dinner at a renown French restaurant, with a major American pharmaceutical firm (currently ranking 7th worldwide), which had a research contract with a Japanese firm. Those present were the American corporation's CEO, executive VP, head of R&D, as well as the president and executives of Mitsubishi petro-chemical firm, as well as myself (at the time a section man-

と応えると、「なぜ？」と問われたので、こともあろうに「とてもユダヤ的だから (It's very Jewish!)」と答えてしまった。皆の目が一斉に私に向かうのを感じた。「ああ、とてもジューシーだから (Sorry, It's juicy)」。私が先方の米国製薬会社の役員とファストネームで会話しているのを聞いていてロンドンのシティーで鍛えた三菱の黒川社長が、隣の私にそっと名刺をくれた。先方のスタッフと勘違いされたらしい。「社長、私は社員です」と言うと、大畑専務も「えっ、うちの人だったの」と。なんとなく嬉しい気分だった。宴が終わると社長は私に「今夜は会社の車で帰りなさい」と、満足げに微笑んだ。

　その夏米国を訪問したら、かのR&D担当VPが「私の家に遊びに来ない？　見せたいものがあるんだ」と言うので訪ねた。なんと、庭にはハニーメロンが大きな果実をつけているではないか。「日本のマスクメロンほどではなくても、米国のメロンもハニーなんだ」と彼は言った。それは賑やかで華やいだ楽しいディナーであった。おかげで、難題もスラスラ解決され、楽しい出張となった。

　1980年代、"グローバリゼーション"という言葉が"インターナショナル"とは別の意味で使われはじめた。宇宙飛行士が言った「地球は青かった」という、あの地球のイメージによく似ている。"グローバリゼーション"の波は私にも及び、欧米の各社から面白いほど誘いがあったが、結局私の条件①長期戦略の保障。結果として15年の契約を結ぶこと、②日本で成功するためには、日本への適応性"adaptability（郷に入っては郷に従え）"を尊重すること、③筑波に研究所を設立すること、をのんでくれたDr. T. クーパーが率いる米国アップジョン社（Upjohn and Company）にお世話になることにした。入社したときは最初の交渉から一年が過ぎていた。当時はよき時代でもあった。

ager). When the dinner was going into the dessert course, the executive VP asked "Toshi, what would you recommend?" I responded with "I think the Japanese musk melon would be good." he asked "Why?" I happened to answer "It's very Jewish!" Needless to say, suddenly all eyes were on me. I immediately corrected, "Sorry, its juicy." The gentleman seated next to me was Mitsubishi's great president, known to have been honed in London's City, silently slipped me his business card. He was mistaken that I was a staff of the other side, because I was talking with them by First name. After the dinner, this president came to me and while smiling in satisfaction with my friendly business conversation with Americans, and said "Take the company car home tonight."

That summer while visiting the United Sates, the head for R&D (CSO) offered "Why don't you come to my home, I have something to show you." Taking up the invitation, and upon arriving at his home, I found in his garden a honey melon of an impressive size. Although it does not compare to the Japanese musk melon, my host states that in the U.S., the melon is honey. The dinner that followed was both lively and beautiful. Adding to this, corporate issues were easily and effortlessly solved, making my business trip a happy and successful experience.

In the 1980s, the phrase 'globalization' with a different meaning than 'international, was being widely used. An astronaut said "The Earth is blue." That image of the Earth is very similar to the 'globalization' phrase. Globalization is a process by which the experiences of everyday life, marked by the sharing of goods and ideas, are becoming standardized around the world, whereas International merely means reaching beyond national boundaries affecting two or more nations. The tide of globalization was surging toward me as well. I was receiving so many offers from western multination firms that it was getting absurd. I decided to establish three terms to those who offered me positions within their organizations. The first term was the guarantee of a long-term strategy ? resulting in a 15 year contract. The second term was an adaptability toward Japan, which would be required to succeed in Japan. This is similar to the expression 'When in Rome, do as the Roman's do." The third term was to

Dr. クーパーは、コーネル大学の医学部長、ワインバーガー教育福祉庁長官時代の福祉担当次官を務め、アップジョン社の会長兼CEOとしてはファミリー以外の最初の人でもあった。Dr. クーパーが就任して迎えたアップジョンでの初めてのクリスマスの時、本社のデコレーションは一変した。本社ビルの大きなクリスマス・レース (X-mas wreath) が消えたのである。当時、私は米国アップジョン研究所の7人のVPのうちの1人（日本とアジア担当）であったが、皆がうらやむほどに、Dr. クーパーには目をかけてもらった。Dr. クーパーの父上はロシアからのユダヤ系移民であったが、クーパー夫人はキリスト教徒である。氏は小柄で、いつも笑顔を絶やさない人だが、一度雷が落ちると皆が震え上がるような決断の人でもあった。学界、ワシントンDCにも太い人脈を持ち、産官学の申し子のような存在だった。

建設現場にて(1987年)

アップジョン筑波研究所

establish a research facility in Tsukuba. Dr. T. Cooper of the U.S. pharmaceutical firm Upjohn accepted all three terms, resulting in my joining this company. It had been one year since starting negotiations. Looking back, that period was a good era.

Dr. Cooper was at one time Dean of Medical School of Cornell University, and during the tenure of Casper Weinberger as Secretary of Health, Education and Welfare, he served as Under Secretary of Welfare. Dr. Cooper was the first Upjohn president and CEO to be appointed outside of the Upjohn family. Dr. Cooper established his mark on the culture of The Upjohn Company. The first Christmas for Dr. Cooper at Upjohn, he completely changed the decorations at headquarters. The huge Christmas wreath had disappeared. During this period I was one of the seven VPs at U.S. Upjohn Research facilities, being responsible for Upjohn Pharmaceutical LTD. He took great interest and attention as to what I was doing to the envy of my colleagues. Dr. Cooper's father was a Jewish immigrant from Russia; however, his wife was Christian. He was a small built man, good natured with an ever-present smile, but when it was necessary, could drop bolts of lightning of decisions that would leave people trembling. He possessed an established network within the academic and political circle of Washington D.C. and truly embodied the spirit of industry, government and academia.

In summary, as can be seen from these examples, the First Command-ment of becoming an internationally minded person is to be ever aware of the cultural background of the people and countries with whom you are dealing.

Dr. T. Cooper

第2話

グローバリゼーション──国境を越えて

　グローバリゼーションとは、ヒト・モノ・カネが国境を越えて自由に行き交うことである。そのグローバリゼーションを迎え撃つのが、地域・国特有の文化といえる。文化を超えてシステム化できるもの、カスタム化できる事柄などは容易に受け入れられ、グローバル化が進む。

　グローバリゼーションについては、日本は受け身であることが多い。しかし、日本発のグローバリゼーションがヨーロッパ文化に大きな影響を与えたことは記憶に新しい。18〜19世紀の浮世絵や陶器である。また、日本にもグローバル思考で、海外進出(貿易とその拠点)を果たそうとした人もいる。平清盛(1118〜1181年)と織田信長(1534〜1582年)である。面白いことに共に出自は平家である。時が早過ぎたのか。

　医薬品研究開発のグローバル化については、解説する必要もないし、もはや聞きたくもないであろう。そこで、最近頻繁に使われるようになり、日常語ともなった"ドラッグラグ"(注)について触れたい。ドラッグラグが日常語となることで医薬品に対する世の関心が高まり、省益を超えた政府の政策や、医薬品医療機器総合機構の充実に功を奏したのはありがたいことである。

　しかし、ドラッグラグがあるから日本の医療体制はおかしいというの

The Second Narrative
Globalization beyond National Borders

Globalization is where people, merchandise and currency freely cross borders, extending beyond only politics and religions. When endeavoring into the realm of globalization, we are quickly reminded of the existence of the various international regions and countries, all possessing their individually unique cultures. Even within this backdrop of cultural differences, there are matters that can rather easily undergo the process of being systemized or customized across the cultural differences to eventually become accepted, thus, globalization goes on.

When speaking of globalization, Japan, in many aspects can be viewed as passive. However, it was not that long ago that Japan contributed its share to globalization significantly, at the time, influencing Europe. This occurred during the 18th and 19th century through 'Ukiyo-e' (wood block prints) and ceramic arts. There were iconic Japanese historical figures who possessed the spirit of globalization, actively entering the foreign market, and opening specific locations to become vibrant export-import trade centers, such as Taira, Kiyomori (1118~1181), and Oda, Nobunaga (1534~1582). It is quite interesting to note that they both share linage to the legendary Heike clan. Perhaps they were both far ahead of the times.

I strongly believe that there is no need to go into, or comment on the subject of globalization of pharmaceutical research and development, and suspect that there are those who would rather not hear of this further. Thus, I will proceed to touch upon a phrase that is so frequently used that it has become an everyday expression? 'Drug Lag' (first introduced by Professor

は、本質を見極めていない短絡的な表現といえる。日本には国民皆保険という世界に類を見ない医療保険制度がある。私はドラッグラグという言葉が一人歩きするのは嫌いである。産官学が絡む話であるが、世界同時開発（SGD: Simultaneous Global Development）が進まない限り、ドラッグラグの解決は実現しない。ちなみに私は2006年に世界医薬品庁（WDO: World Drug Organization）の設立を提案している（Toshi Kobayashi, Expert Opinion Drug Discovery（2006）1（3）205 / London）。申請するのが1カ所ならば、その申請への回答も1カ所で済まされるからである。

　ドラッグラグは、"申請ラグ"と"審査ラグ"が原因となって起きている。申請ラグについてだが、すべての製品を、グローバルに開発しようとする企業などはありえない。グローバルに開発することを決めた製品についての日米欧の申請時期を比較してみるとわかることである。審査ラグについては、日米欧の産官学の努力により、日本においても審査の工程表（review metrics）に基づく評価が実現した。客観性をもって評価できるラグ（遅れ）である。PDUFA-IV（Prescription Drug User Fee Act-IV）でREMS（Risk Evaluation and Mitigation Strategies）を取り入れた米国（FDA：Food and Drug Administration、アメリカ食品医薬局）を見ると、日米どちらが遅れを負うのか興味のあるところである。

　ここでグローバリゼーションに関連して、日米政府間の対話について触れておきたい。日米政権下における医療関連対話は、いわゆる1984年に始まったMOSS協議（Market-Oriented Sector Selective Negotiations）以来、延々と名称を変えて続いてきたが、昨年（2011年）は開かれなかった。米国では、オバマ政権の医療政策（参考：小林利彦「オバマ医療政策の全貌——恩恵と痛み」『製剤機械技術研究会誌』、Vol.19 No.3、2010年）

Thomas of Emory University, U.S.). It was through the repeated use of this phrase that heightened the attention to one of the prominent issues surrounding Japan's pharmaceutical industry. The expression not only manifested attention, it also proved to be generator in motivating proactive cross-ministry interaction to introduce new medical policies, but the most noted contribution of the 'Drug Lag' expression was that it led to the establishment of the Pharmaceuticals and Medical Devices Agency (PMDA : US FDA-like).

However, just because 'Drug Lag' existed in Japan, it would be mistaken to conclude that the Japanese medical system is flawed. If this is the case, then it would have to be said that the real issue was not properly identified and the phrase would simply be expressing a short-sighted view. Japan is noted for its health care system that is one of the best in the world, providing the Japanese public with universal medical insurance coverage. Personally I dislike the way that the phrase 'Drug Lag' took off on its own. If Simultaneous Global Development (SGD) does not progress in Japan, although this would involve the industry, government and academia, there will be no resolution to the problem. For instance, in 2006 I submitted a proposal to establish the World Drug Organization (WDO) : (Toshi Kobayashi, Expert Opinion Drug Discovery (2006) 1 (3) 205/London), in which I presented that if an application is submitted to one location/WDO, the response of approval and licensing would also be conducted at the same location/WDO with one time for the worldwide use..

'Drug Lag' occurs due to 'Application Lag' and 'Review Lag'. In the face of the 'Application Lag', it is inconceivable for a company to conduct development for all of its products in Japan according to the global priority orders. It is easily recognizable by comparing application timings in Japan, the United States and Europe of all products selected for global development. So,' Application Lag 'will not be easily eliminated. The 'Review Lag', however, through the efforts of industry/government/academia of Japan, the U.S and Europe, can be measured because review metrics were established also in Japan. Thus, although existent, the current lag can be given a favorable appraisal with ob-

をめぐる中間選挙（民主党の敗北）があり、日本でも参議院選挙（民主党の敗北）にぶつかり、多忙だったからだろう。しかし、2011年に向けて2010年11月のオバマ・菅会談で日米政府間会議の枠組みが決まった。日米経済調和対話（U.S.-Japan Economic Harmonization Initiative）である。医療関係もここで取り上げられる。産業界の意見も十分議論されることになるだろう。

（注）ドラッグラグという言葉は米国で初めて使われた。サリドマイドの副作用が問題となった1960年代、米国では安全性にあまりにも慎重になり医薬品の承認が遅れた。エイズ問題が起きた時（1980年代）には、打つ手がなく、死の病とされた。これに業を煮やしたエドワード・ケネディー上院議員が発破を掛け、その承認の遅れを取り戻すために使われた言葉である。一方日本では、欧米と比較して承認の遅れを示す言葉として使用されている。

浮世絵
© tsuyoshit - Fotolia.com

中国の磁器
© momo_leif - Fotolia.com

jectivity. Let us take a look at the United States with their Prescription Drug User Fee Act–IV (PDUFA–IV), which adopted the Risk Evaluation and Mitigation Strategy (REMS), it would be interesting to see whether the 'lag' label will be worn by Japan or the United States.

Here I would like to touch upon globalization dialogue between the Japanese and American governments. Health care related dialogue between the administrations of the U.S. and Japan, starting in 1985 within the Market Oriented Sector Selective (MOSS) Negotiations, although the title of the meetings have undergone changes, had consecutively been held, but it was not held for the year 2010. In the United States there was the midterm election focusing on health care policy of the Obama administration (reference: Toshi Kobayashi/A Comprehensive Look at Obama's Health Care Policy —Its Benefits and Pain— Japan Society of Pharmaceutical Machinery and Engineering Journal Vol. 19 No. 3 (2010), and referring to the fact of resulting in losses for the Democratic Party, adding to this, Japan's Upper House held its election, also resulting in the Democratic Party of Japan losing seats, everyone was probably too busy campaigning to hold negotiations. However, in 2011, a meeting was held between President Obama and Prime Minister Kan which resulted in establishing the framework for the Japan-U.S. government talks which is the U.S. —Japan Economic Harmonization Initiative, in which health care related issues are to be addressed. I predict that there will be a great deal of debate centering on the opinions put forward by the industry.

第3話
日本、"Executive Pipeline"を

　医薬産業では、企業の価値を"プロダクト・パイプライン（Product Pipeline）"の充実に求められがちであるが、"人材パイプライン（Executive Pipeline）"も同じ重さの価値があるのではないだろうか。GE（General Electric Company）の前CEOであるラリー・ウェルチ（Larry Welch）が言った「一流は一流を雇うが、二流は二流しか雇えない」により、自明である。

　十戒といえばモーゼの十戒に思いを馳せる。しかしここで私はユダヤ（教）の教義を論ずる心算は毛頭ない。ただユダヤの人々が紀元前6世紀のバビロンの捕囚以来、今日に至るまで"民（バーチャル国家）"として永らえてこられたのは何故であろうか。それはモーゼがユダヤの民を連れて、エジプトを出て（紀元前1200年頃といわれている）シナイにいたる40年の厳しい道中、しかも最終的には民が100万人単位にもなった中で、一人ひとりが自らを律することにより連帯を保てた戒律を、モーゼ後の人々が守ってきたからに他ならない。

　混沌とする現代社会の中で、自らを律するにあたって"十戒"というより"10のお話"として今でも役に立つのではないかと思う次第である。自らを律することのできる人々の集まりとして、属する組織（産官学を問わず）にも役に立つことができるというわけだ。

The Third Narrative

Japan Inc. Strengthening the "Executive Pipeline"

In the pharmaceutical industry, there is a tendency to measure the value of the corporation by its products and how ample their pipeline is. However, I believe that the quality of their management pipeline ? Executive Pipeline ? holds an equally important value to a corporation. This is clear from a quote from former GE CEO Jack Welch, "First rate people hire first-rate people; second rate managers hire second-rate people."

When referring to the 10 Commandments, many will envision "The Ten Commandments of Moses". I have absolutely no intention of starting a debate into the religious teachings of the Jewish faith. However, looking back into history, from the 6th century BC, when they were enslaved by the Babylonians, to the present, how did the Jewish people strongly sustain their identity within a [virtual nation]? Perhaps it all began with Moses when he led the Israelites out of Egypt (said to be in 1200BC), embarking upon the Exodus to Mount Sinai. This was a grueling endeavor lasting 40 years, and the sheer number of people reaching the millions, only made possible through a combination of Moses' ability as an executive (leader) and each individual's self-disciplinary conduct within established principles which have been honored even after Moses.

In today's chaotic society, the "Ten Commandments", or shall I say the "Ten Narratives", may be of assistance in practicing self-discipline. An organization, regardless of its nature (industry/government/academia) will ultimately benefit through having people who are capable of practicing good self-discipline.

もともと、ユダヤの律法（Torah）には613の戒めがある。365の否定的戒め（negative commandments：〜してはならない）と248の肯定的戒め（positive commandments：〜しなくてはならない）である。その中から選ばれたのが10の戒めであり、通常モーゼの十戒といわれる。その他の十戒としてはキリスト教プロテスタント派の十戒がよく見かけられるが、ここではユダヤ教（旧約聖書）の10の戒めで話を進めたい。キリスト教プロテスタントの十戒はユダヤ教の第1の戒めを外し、第2の戒めを第1と第2に分けただけで、内容的にはまったく変わらない。キリスト教が外した第1の戒めとは"I am the Lord your God.（私は主、あなた方の神である）"である。これは確かに、戒めとは異質に見える。第1の戒めとは何であったのか。それはモーゼが神から授けられた"mission statement（天命の声名）"だと、筆者は解釈している。その"mission（天命）"とは何か。それは第4話に譲りたい。

　次話以降の参考のために、ここでユダヤ教の喜怒哀楽の情について、キリスト教の教え（「自分に憎しみを持っている人も愛せよ」など）との違いを紹介しておきたい。ユダヤ教では「愛はいつもよいこととは限らないし、憎しみはいつも悪いばかりではない」「社会的制裁（罰）を受ける悪(ワル)を憎むのは、悪いことではない」など、意外に現実的である。

　ここからは十戒の各戒について、筆者の体験を踏まえながら進めていきたい。ちなみにアーサー・クルツウェール（Arthur Kurzweil）による英訳'The Ten Commandments'（参考：www.arthurkurzweil.com）は以下の通りである。

1. I am the Lord your God.
2. You shall have no other gods before me. You shall not make for yourself an

The Torah of the Jewish faith consists of 613 commandments. There are 365 negative, or thou shall not, commandments, and 248 positive, or thou shall, commandments. It is from these numerous commandments that the "Ten Commandments" were selected and often referred to as "The Ten Commandments of Moses". The Ten Commandments are frequently referred to, and seen in the Christian and Protestant faiths, but I would like to further go into detail about the Ten Commandments of the Jewish faith in the old testament of the Bible. The difference seen in the Ten Commandments of this Jewish faith, is that the First Commandment has been removed and the Second Commandment has been divided into the First and Second. The contents do not change at all. However, in the Christian faith, the First Commandment is "I am the Lord your God. . . ", this phrase does not come across as a lesson, or discipline to be followed. Then what was to be conveyed through the First Commandment? My understanding is that it was a "mission statement" given to Moses by God. What was that "mission"? Considering the editorial space, I will approach this within the next narrative. However, God relied on Moses' leadership ability to execute the mission.

As reference for the next narrative, I will touch upon the difference between the Christian faith and its merciful approach to the various emotions we possess, (example: Love your enemies, bless them that curse you, do good to them that hate you. . . .) and that of the Jewish faith. In the Jewish faith, love is not always a good emotion, and hate is not always a bad emotion. When someone has broken the law, and receives punishment of a civil society, the negative emotions toward the convicted are accepted. This concept is surprisingly realistic.

I would like to proceed with touching upon each of the Ten Commandments, based upon experience. The following are The Ten Commandments of the Old Testment which was translated by Arthur Kurzweil.

1. I am the Lord your God.
2. You shall have no other gods before me; You shall not make for yourself an

idol.

3. Do not take the name of the Lord in vain.

4. Remember and observe the Sabbath and keep it holy.

5. Honor your father and mother.

6. You shall not kill / murder.

7. You shall not commit adultery.

8. You shall not steal.

9. You shall not bear false witness against your neighbor.

10. You shall not covet your neighbor's wife and house.

idol.

3. Do not take the name of the Lord in vain.
4. Remember and observe the Sabbath and keep it holy.
5. Honor your father and mother.
6. You shall not kill/murder.
7. You shall not commit adultery.
8. You shall not steal.
9. You shall not bear false witness against your neighbor.
10. You shall not covet your neighbor's wife and house.

第4話
自らの天命を自覚せよ

　第1の戒"I am the Lord your God.（私は主(シュ)、あなた方の神である）"は、ユダヤの神からモーゼへの"ミッション・ステートメント（Mission Statement：天命の声名）"であったと筆者は理解している。だからこそ、モーゼより千数百年以降、ユダヤ教の宗旨変えを迫ったキリストを主とするキリスト教が第1の戒を外したのは、よく理解できる（参照：第1章第3話）。

　"天命の声名（Mission Statement）"と"天命（Mission）"は、現代社会のリーダーにとっても、また個人にとっても、最も重要なことの1つである。

　では、モーゼにとって天命（Mission）とは何であったのか。それは、出エジプト（Egypt Exodus）であった。ユダヤの民の430年に及ぶエジプトでの奴隷生活に終止符を打つことであった。ユダヤ奴隷の長男としてエジプトに生まれたモーゼは、奇しくも失うべき命を川辺で王家の姫君に救われて、時のファラオですら認める優れた王子として成長した。

　しかし、たまたまモーゼはユダヤ奴隷を虐げるエジプト人を殺してしまい、父祖の地カナンに逃れることとなる。後、義兄のアーロンと共に、エジプトのユダヤ奴隷の解放こそ天命（Mission）である、との"神の命令

The Fourth Narrative
The Mission——God's will.

When I read the First Commandment, "I am the Lord your God" my understanding is that this was a "Mission Statement" to Moses from the Jewish faith's God. Thus, it is understandable why the Christians do not include this particular Commandment. (Refer to the Third Narrative).

The Mission Statement and the Mission is one of the most important principles for a leader or an individual within today's society.

Then, what was Moses' Mission within the Mission Statement? It was the Exodus from Egypt, freeing the Israelites from Egypt, and putting an end to 430 years of slavery. Born to a Hebrew mother, at a time when there was a command that all male Hebrew children were to be killed, Moses was sent adrift on a small basket down the Nile River where he was discovered and adopted by the Pharaoh's daughter. Reaching adulthood Moses became the younger brother to the future Pharaoh, a prince.

Moses, seeing an Egyptian beating a Hebrew slave, killed the Egyptian and fled to his ancestral home land of Canaan. Later with his elder brother Aaron, Moses embarked for Egypt, grudgingly accompanied by his wife and children, to fulfill the "Mission" and the "directive" to free the Israelites. Moses at the age of 80, started the Exodus from Egypt which took 40 years to end.

When referring to "Mission", I cannot but help remember George Merck. The grandson of Merck KGaA (1827) founder Emanuel Merck. George, in 1891 founded Merck & Co. in New York and for 25 years (1925~1950) served as president and contributed in building Merck. His "Mission" was

(directive)"を受け、しぶしぶ決意して妻子を連れてエジプトに向かった。時に齢80歳といわれたモーゼは、"出エジプト (Egypt Exodus)"を40年の歳月をかけ、実現したのである。

　天命 (Mission) といえば、独メルク社 (Merck KGaA: 1827年～) の創業者エマニエル・メルク (Emanuel Merck) の孫であるジョージ・メルク (George Merck) を思い出す。彼は1891年、米国ニューヨークに米メルク社 (Merck&Co.) を設立し、25年間 (1925～1950年) 社長として、メルク社をグローバル化させた人物である。

　彼のMission（天命）ともいうべき「医薬品は人々のためにあり、利益のためにあるのではない。このことを忘れなければ利益は必ずついてくる（We try never to forget that medicine is for the people. It is not for the profits. The profits follow, and if we have remembered that, they（profits）have never failed to appear.)」は至言である。

　また私は、米国メルク社の中興の祖ともいうべきロイ・ヴァージロス (Roy Vagelos) と1976年に会う機会があった。メルク研究所所長 (President of Merck Research Laboratories) になったばかりの彼は、大きなオフィスに机1つで将来への抱負を語ってくれた。後、2005年にはワシントンDCで講演をし、戦後、中国にワクチン製造と技術移転を無償で提供したことを語った。中国の子ども達の感染症による悲惨さを実体験したのだという。ジョージ・メルク (George Merck) の天命 (Mission) を守ってきた証である。その時いただいた彼のサイン入り 'Medicine, Science and Merck' は筆者の本棚にある。

　さて、ここで年初来違う展開を見せているライバル同士のメルク

"We try never to forget that medicine is for the people. It is not for the profits. The profits follow, and if we have remembered that, they (the profits) have never failed to appear."

In 1976 I had the wonderful opportunity to meet with Roy Vagelos who was in what can be called the middle management of U.S.'s Merck & Co. He had just become president of MRL (Merck Research Laboratories) and seated at the one desk in a spacious office, started to share his future aspirations with me. Later, in 2005 I heard him speak at a function in Washington D.C. In his speech, he reflected on his experience after the war, how a free technology hand-over was conducted to China to manufacture vaccines. This was most likely the result of his first-hand experience of seeing the desolate conditions of the Chinese children afflicted with contagious diseases. It was also proof that the "Mission" laid out by George Merck was honored and prevailed. At that time, he gave me a signed copy of "Medicine, Science and Merck", which holds a proud position in my bookshelf.

Now, let us take a look at how two rivals, Merck and Pfizer, have taken different paths to growth. Respectively their CEOs are Ken Frazier, 55 years old, with a legal background, and Ian Read, 57 years old, background as CPA with engineering. This proved to be a challenging year for both gentlemen; Merck purchased Schering-Plough and Pfizer purchased Wyeth. It is however their approaches to research and development, that the difference is evident. Mr. Frazier, although he lowered the cost for operations, did not contain R&D costs. On the other hand, Mr. Read decided on a drastic measure of making a 30% reduction to R&D. I would like to see how, not only the leader but also the employees, acknowledge their "Mission" and the outcome of the different strategies to implement their mission.

(Merck)とファイザー（Pfizer）を眺めてみたい。それぞれCEOがケン・フレージャー（Ken Frazier：1954年〜、弁護士出身）、イアン・リード（Ian Read：1953年〜、公認会計士・エンジニア）に変わり、それぞれシェリング‐プラウ（Schering-Plough）、ワイエス（Wyeth）を買収してチャレンジングな年を迎えた。しかし研究開発に対する両者の考えは、かなり違う。フレジャー氏は、事業の下方修正をしても研究開発コストを据え置いたが、片やリード氏は、研開費30％削減という荒療治を決断した。リーダーもさることながら、どちらの社員が自らの天命（Mission）を自覚して、目をより輝かせるのか注目したい。

> Medicine, Science and Merck
>
> P. ROY VAGELOS
> LOUIS GALAMBOS

著者謹呈

Statue of Moses, vintage engraving
© Morphart - Fotolia.com

第5話

リーダー、「透明な頑固さ」を持て

　モーゼ第2の戒めには、"You shall not recognize other gods before me.（私に先んじて他の神々を認めてはならない）"にはじまり、"You shall not make for yourself an idol.（あなた方は、自らを偶像化してはならない）"そして、"For I am a jealous God（私は、a jealous Godであるから）"と続く。

　ユダヤの人々は、戒めの前半である"神は1人である"こと、しかもその神が"a jealous God（独占欲の強い神）"であることを伝統的に認めてきている。"a jealous God"については、神には言葉がないので人間の文字にすると"jealous（独占欲の強い）"となると説いてきた。そして、これを日本語にするにあたって筆者は大変に悩んだ。つらつら思案し、"自信に満ちた透明な頑固さ"と解釈した。

　出エジプトという天命（Mission）のために、40年の歳月をかけたモーゼは、道中どのようにして100万人単位の同胞を統率して、無事シナイ（Sinai）に戻るのか。常に迷いと闘い、都度教えを乞うたユダヤの神とモーゼに特に必要であったのが、"自信に満ちた透明な頑固さ"であったのではないかと思うからである。

　"The Lord Your God"は固有名詞である。そこで、固有名詞である皆様個人が「私は自信に満ちた透明な頑固さを持っている」と考えてみてほ

The Fifth Narrative

A Leader's Fundamental Necessity, Clear Determination Filled with Confidence

The first segment of the Second Commandment of Moses, "You shall not recognize other gods before me." and "You shall not make for yourself an idol", "For I am a jealous God."

The Jewish people have traditionally accepted the first segment of the Second Commandment, which states that there is only one God, and that this God is a jealous God. It has been said that within the phrase "a jealous God", the word 'jealous' was written as such by human beings, for God did not communicate with a specific written language. To reflect this phrase in the Japanese language, I did some serious contemplation and came to the conclusion of "Clear Determination, Filled with Confidence".

For Moses to fulfill his 'mission', which took 40 years involving hundreds of thousands of people, he had to ensure that they shared the same aspiration, and safely returned to the Sinai. This endeavor was certainly not without the constant battle with doubt. What was presumably necessary for Moses, through his prayers to the Jewish god, was to possess 'Clear Determination, Filled with Confidence'.

The Lord Your God is a name. As each and every one of us has a name, I hope that each individual thinks in terms of "I possess clear determination filled with confidence". As well as imagine that you are in a revered position and are responsible for combining, or managing many people. If you place yourself in Moses' place, with the insurmountable difficulties he faced, and conceiving his emotions, these words will start to shine with meaning. The word 'Clear' is important. It is through clarity that corporate battles can be

しい。しかも多くの人々を束ねていかなくてはならない長たる立場であったら、と。苦難に立ち向かうモーゼの心境になってみれば、この言葉は生き生きと輝きを放つ。"透明さ"が重要である。透明であってこそ、さわやかに競争に勝ちリーダーの位置を得、さらにその組織も適切な形（right sizing：大きいばかりが能ではない）で安定するのである。

　ここで最近話題となった"透明な頑固さ"と"不透明な頑固さ"の例を示したい。

　フランク・ランプル（Frank Lampl）は、1926年、チェコのユダヤ系農場主の息子に生まれ、アウシュヴィッツでは家族で1人だけ生き残り、プラハの春でも共産党員ではなかったため迫害を受けて、オックスフォードに留学中の息子を頼りに、着の身着のままの状態で妻ブランカ（Blanka）と英国に逃れた。時に42歳。ロンドンでボーヴィス（Bovis）社を興し、世界最大級の建設大手に育てた。彼は公平さと面倒見のよさを信条とし、自らの会社を語るに「私〜（I...）」ではなく、常に「我々〜（We...）」と話したという。そして、かなり頑固（Hard-nosed）でもあった。ボーヴィス社の手掛けた建築には、ロンドンのカナリー埠頭、パリ郊外のユーロディズニー、日本でもおなじみのクアラルンプールのペトロナスタワーなどがある。1990年には、英国でナイトの称号を得て、2010年、84歳で没した。

　逆に不透明さの典型としてバーナード・マドフ（Bernard Madoff）があげられる。1938年、ニューヨークのクイーンズにある商売繁盛しているユダヤ系スポーツ用品店の息子として誕生。妻・ルース（Ruth）の助けも得て、カレッジを卒業。その後は修理屋のような仕事をしていた。やがて、弟・ピーター（Peter）と合法的に資産運営をするためにブルミ

won with grace and dignity, and secures an individual as a leader, as well as provide an organization with proper size (size is not everything) and stability.

Here I would like to give examples of 'clear determination' and 'unclear determination', which have recently been talked about.

Frank Lamp was born in 1926 to a Czech-Jew farmer. Sadly, of his entire family he was the only one to survive the Auschwitz prison camp. Later during the Prague Spring, he suffered persecution for not being a member of the Communist Party. Relying on his son, who was studying at Oxford; he left for England with his wife Blanka, with only the clothes on his back. He was 42 years old at the time. Once in London he established Bovis, which he built into one of the world's largest construction firms. He was known for his 'fairness and consideration' which became his motto. When referring or speaking about his company, he would not use the term "I. . . ." but would always start out with "We. . . ." However he was also known for being very determined, or 'hard-nosed'. Among the many projects constructed by Bovis, are London's Canary Pier, Euro Disney located just outside of Paris, and Kuala Lumpur's Petrona Star Tower, which is well known in Japan as well. In 1990 the British knighted him. He passed away in 2010 at the age of 84.

A perfect example of 'unclear determination' would be Bernard Madoff. He was born in 1938 in New York's Queens to a successful Jewish sports shop owner. With assistance from his wife Ruth, he graduated from college, and later worked as a kind of repairman. He, along with his brother Peter, established BLMIS, a company that legally conducted asset management, thus, entering the financial sector. BLMIS grew and in 1990 Bernard became the Chairman of NASDAQ. It was from this point that he, along with three 'unclear' associates after the discovery of the Ponzi scheme, involving many investors, was arrested in November, 2008. Only after his arrest, did his family learn of what he was involved in. It is said that 'unclearness' started with the ethnic bonding with his associates and tax evasion. In 2009, the court handed down a sentence of 150 years. Moses would have said, "Long ago, you would not have had it so easy".

ス（BLMIS）社を設立し、金融業界に入った。ブルミス社は成長し、1990年にはナスダックの会長にまでなった。しかしこの頃から、不透明な仲間3人と組んで、多くの投資家を巻き込み、2008年11月に650億ドルの不正運営が発覚して、逮捕となる。不正運営については家族もこの時初めて知ったという。彼が不透明になったきっかけは、仲間とのエスニック意識と脱税にあったという。2009年には服役150年の刑が確定した。モーゼは言うであろう「昔ならこんなものでは済まない！」と。

Newly developed "City of London"

第6話
リーダー、自らを偶像化してはならない

　第2の戒の後半部 "You shall not make for yourself a carved image.（あなた方は、自らを偶像化してはならない）"からすると、キリスト教の教会がキリスト像を祭っているのは、破戒である。しかしキリストを主(シュ)と呼び神格化したのは、キリスト後のキリスト教徒でありキリスト自身ではない。キリストは、法然（1133～1212年、浄土宗）、親鸞（1173～1262年、浄土真宗）やルター（Martin Luther：1483～1546年、キリスト教プロテスタント派）などの宗教改革の先駆者であったのだろう。キリスト教が世界最大の宗教となったのには、それなりの理由があったはずである。真意は"偶像化"にあるのではなく、"信念の拠り所としての象徴を具体化"することであったというべきか。

　考えるに、自らを偶像化して永遠に続いた例はあまりないのではないだろうか。宗教ではないが、ローマ帝国の皇帝しかりである。ただ、あとに続く人達が先達や創業者の考えを社訓のようなかたちで象徴化することは多々ある。三菱における岩崎家、ロスチャイルドのバウアー家がその例である。

　製薬業界では、筆者が勤めたアップジョン社では、W.E.アップジョン氏(W.E. Upjohn)の "Keep the Quality Up（いつまでも高品質を維持せよ）"と共に尊敬した。また、イーライリリー社では、リリー大佐(Colonel

The Sixth Narrative
Leader, No Self-Idolization

The later segment of the Second Commandment, "You shall not make for yourself a carved image" when looking at it from the point of view of the Christian faith, where the image of Christ is prominent in its churches, this is a transgression. It was the Christians, after Christ, who refer to Christ as the Lord, and have his image deified. Christ, as with Hohnen (1133-1212, Johdo Sect in Buddhism), Shinran (1173-1262, Johdo Shin Sect in Buddhism) and Luther (1483-1546, Protestant) was most likely the forerunner of religious revolutionaries. There must be a reason why Christianity has become one of the largest religious faiths in the world. It is not to take on the form of idolization, but as a clearly defined figure to support one's beliefs, and prayers.

Thinking back, it is extremely rare that an individual be idolized and that to continue for eternity. Although not a religion, the Caesars of the Roman Empire might be in this category. There are many examples of the social phenomena of people who remember their ancestors, or founders through the practice of idolization. Mitsubishi's Iwasaki family, and the Rothschild's Bower family are examples of this.

In the pharmaceutical industry, at W.E. Upjohn, where I was employed and greatly respected, there was the motto of "Keep the Quality Up". As well, at Eli Lilly and Company, again where I was a part of, and came to hold great respect for, operated on a motto from Colonel Lilly, "Integrity, Excellence, and Respect for People". However, in today's business environment, where constant over-night changes in the form of M&A take place, the number of recognized global top-class pharmaceutical manufacturers such as; Pfizer,

Lilly) を"Integrity, Excellence, and Respect for People（誠実さ、卓越性の追求、人の尊重）"と共に尊敬した。しかし、現在のビジネスモデルの急激な変化（M&Aなど）と共に、世界トップクラスの医薬事業で名をとどめるのは、ファイザー、メルク、ロシュ、リリーと数少なくなった。ただし、嘆くことはない。新たに、アムジェン、ジェネンテック、テバなどが生まれている。

さて、"透明な頑固さ"の話に戻りたい。T. エジソンが1889年に創業したGE（General Electric）の会長兼CEOを21年（1981〜2001年）務めたジャック・ウェルチ氏（Jack Welch）である。退任後10年経つ現在もそのイズムの伝道者として妻・スージー（Suzy）とともに現役である。筆者はウェルチ氏を直接知らない。しかし、氏の薫陶よろしきを得た人々を知っている。

その最たる人の1人が、ピーター・レッシャー（Peter Loescher）独シーメンス社のCEO（2007年〜）である。2000年から2004年までヘキストジャパン／アベンティスジャパンの社長として、EFPIA（European Federation of Pharmaceutical Industries and Associations）日本代表としても日本で活躍した。後、アマーシャム社（スウェーデン）を経て、GEの医療・バイオサイエンスの責任者を務めた後、米国メルクの医薬事業本部長（事実上のナンバー2）として迎えられた。

また、2007年には、汚職問題を抱えた独シーメンス社にCEO兼社長として非ドイツ人として初めて招かれた。彼はオーストリア生まれである。筆者は、その時彼が言った言葉が忘れられない。600人のシーメンス幹部は、「あまりに白人が多く、あまりにドイツ人が多く、あまりに男性が多い（Siemens, too white, German and male）」。これぞ非グローバリ

Merck, Roche and Lilly, is but a few. But there is no need to wail and worry, there are also the births of new firms such as; Amgen, Genentech and TEVA

I would like to get back to the topic of 'Clear Determination'. Thomas Edison founded General Electric in 1889, and Jack Welch was its CEO and Chairman for 21 years (1981-2001). Even after 10 years since retiring, he is still conveying the 'ism', and along with his wife Suzie, is active. I don't have the pleasure of actually knowing Mr. Welch; however, I do know many who are testimony to his great tutoring.

The perfect individual to reflect this is Peter Loescher, CEO of German Siemens (2007-present). From the years 2000 to 2004 he was actively operating in Japan as the president of Hoechst Japan/Aventis Japan as well as overseeing EFPIA as its Japan Representative. After which he was with Amersham (Sweden) and went on to become responsible for GE Medical Bioscience, followed by becoming second in command at U.S. Merck through heading its pharmaceutical division.

In 2007, when German Siemens was in the midst of a corruption issue, he became the first non-German to be offered the post of president and CEO. Peter was born in Austria. I cannot forget the words that Peter spoke at that time. Of the 600 Siemens management, he said "Siemens ? too white, German and male." This was real evidence of non-globalization. At the same time he pronounced a 'Year of clean living". For these past several years, with his 'Clear Determination' he has succeeded in gradually increasing the transparency of Siemens.

I sincerely wish for the success of the medical division, along with energy and heavy industries of Siemens to become one of its three pillars of future growth.

ゼーションの典型である。同時に"透明元年 (Year of clean living)"を宣言した。ここ数年、彼の"透明な頑固さ"でシーメンスは徐々に透明さを増している。

医療関係の事業は、エネルギー、重工業と共にシーメンスの三本柱として展開を進めている。成功を望んでやまない。

（注）ピーター・レッシャーでさえ、2013年にはCEOの座を追われている。生き馬の目を抜くとは、この事か。

オランダの風景　　　　　　　　　　　　　　　　　© Lsantilli - Fotolia.com

Amsterdam (1980), together Prof. Henk Timmerman and Prof. Adrian Albert

第7話

自らの言葉を甘く見るな
―― 言葉は消えない、実在する

　モーゼ第3の戒めは"You shall not take the name of the Lord your God in vain.（軽々しく神の名をかたってはいけない）"である。ユダヤの人々の間では、一度話した言葉は、非常に重要な意味を持っている。"真剣そのもの"という伝統があった。我々は、「神に誓って～」などと言って、ケロッと忘れていることが多々ある。しかし、ユダヤの律では「公共の場で不当に言葉で人を傷つけることは、その人を殺すことに等しい」とまで言っている。要するに誓いとか約束は実在するものであって、軽々と使ってはいけないということである。

　アップジョン時代（1980年代～1990年代前半）、ミシガン州カラマズーの本社へ行くと、必ずCEOのDr. クーパー（参照：第1章第1話）を訪ねることにしていた。その朝は「7時に来い」と言うので、6時半に、当時タージマハールと呼ばれていた本社2階の広いフロアーに着いた。すると、誰もいないのにCEO室から小柄なDr. クーパーの大きな声がビンビンと響いてくる。何事かと遠くから覗いて驚く。

　額に拳を当ててCEOの机に肘をつき、激しく降ってくる叱咤にじっと耐えるN氏が居るではないか。N氏は3年前にFDA（Food and Drug Administration、アメリカ食品医薬局）長官代行からアップジョン入りした社内ナンバー3の大物である。当時は、PDUFA（Prescription Drug

The Seventh Narrative

Beware of What You Say, Words Do Not Disappear

Moses' Third Commandment, "You shall not take the name of the Lord your God in vain." To the Jewish people, what is once said carries a great deal of importance. "A serious thing" as it is known traditionally. For our part, we may "Swear to God" and then in many cases, completely forget about it. The principles of the Jewish, if words of injustice are directed to an individual in a public place, it is said to be the equivalent of killing that individual. In short, pledges and promises exist and these are not to be spoken lightly.

During my years with Upjohn (1980-early 1990s), headquarters were located in Kalamazoo, Michigan, and each time I had the opportunity to visit, I would make it a policy to visit CEO Dr. Cooper. That particular morning I was told to come by 7:00, arriving at 6:30. Proceeding to what at the time was referred to as the 'Taj Mahal', the spacious second floor of headquarters, although no one was there I could hear the slight (refer to Narrative Three) Dr. Cooper's voice booming. Wondering what was going on, I took a peek from a distance, and was surprised at what I saw. There, with his fist to his forehead and elbows on the CEO's desk was Mr. MN. bearing the ever escalating blasting pep talk. Three years ago, prior to when he joined Upjohn, Dr . N was a representative for commissioner FDA, and was No. 3 within the firm's management ? a leading executive. At this time, it was before PDUFA (established 1992), the reviews conducted by the FDA were all being delayed, causing international competition strength to diminish. It was during this time that Senator Edward Kennedy (Democrat) was concerned and had started to initiate changes to the FDA (introducing the user-fee act and establishing PDU-

User Fee Act、1992年）施行前であり、FDAの審査が軒並み遅れ、国際競争力が落ちることをエドワード・ケネディー上院議員（Edward Kennedy、民主党）が心配し、FDA改革（PDUFAの制定）に乗り出していた頃である。アップジョンでは、大型戦略品の審査が遅れ、アナリストや投資家から批判が出ていた。N氏が約束（情報提供）したタイミングには間に合わなかったのである。

　この凄まじい光景は、今でも鮮明に蘇る。攻めるも守るも必死！　これが真剣勝負かと肝に銘じた。

　ここで言いたいのは、意思決定の結果が「負」と出た時の責任はだれが取るのか、という問題である。10人の会議で全員で検討しても、決定者は議長の場合が多く、最終的にはどうあれ、全員一致の結果ということになりがちである。意思決定の会議では、"決定者（decision maker、1〜2人）"と"情報提供者（informers）"を明確にすべきである。情報が間違っていれば、責任は決定者でなく情報提供者にある。こんなことがあった。ある開発品の決定会議で、臨床フェーズⅡa（Ph-Ⅱa）の報告があり、臨床フェーズⅡb（Ph-Ⅱb）に進むか否かの討論があった。プロダクトリーダーの説明を受けて"ゴーサイン（go-sign）"が出た。ところが10カ月後の臨床フェーズⅡb会議の場に、そのプロダクトリーダーがいない。「どうしたの？」と聞くと、隣のVP曰く「奴が責任とったのさ」と。臨床フェーズⅡaでの"主観的データ（subjective）"を"客観的データ（objective）"として説明していたのだった。

　Dr. クーパーは後に骨髄腫と診断されて、3カ月で急逝された（1993年春）。発病後取締役会に諮り、氏の退任（寿命）と共にN氏も退任することを条件に、N氏を厚遇することを決めていたのだという。のちに米国

FA). At Upjohn, the review process of a major strategic product was delayed, and criticism from analysts and investors were mounting. The timing of Mr. N's promise (provision of information) was not kept.

I can still clearly remember this horrific scene. The aggressor and defender, mutually desperately holding their positions, this is when I realized what a true serious match was, and have since kept it to heart.

What I would like to say here is, if the decision-made results in a 'loss', who is going to take the responsibility? Let us say that in a meeting, in which 10 people take place, and all participants review and weigh the issues, in most cases it is the chair of the meeting who makes the decision. Whatever the results, it will be considered a decision reached unanimously by all.

In a decision-making meeting, we have to be clear that there are one or two decision makers, and the existence of those who provide information, or the informers. If the information is mistaken, the responsibility is not on the decision-makers but those who provided the unreliable information. Let me share an incident. At a product development decision-making meeting, there was a report on the Ph-IIa, a debate followed as to determine whether or not to proceed into Ph-IIb. The product leader gave a fine explanation which resulted in a 'go-ahead'. Ten months later at the Ph-IIb meeting, the leader was nowhere to be seen, I asked "What happened?" The VP seated next to me replied "He took the responsibility." This was all due to the product leader giving a fine explanation of the Ph-IIa subjective data as if it was the objective data.

Later Dr. Cooper was diagnosed with myeloma, and within three months passed away in the spring of 1993. After the diagnosis, an executive board meeting was called to weigh this unfortunate development. Then, Dr. Cooper requested of the board that when he retired/died, Mr. MN would retire also with a special retirement bonus. Later Mr. MN would become chairman of U.S. Pharmacopeia. Then I was able to learn these facts directly from Mr. MN during a visit to Washington D.C. In a letter from Dr. Cooper dated March 23, 1993, to me, he thanked me for taking Tsukuba Shrine Health

薬局方（U.S. Pharmacopeia）の会長になったN氏から直接ワシントンDCで話を家内と共に、聞く機会があった。1993年3月23日付のDr. クーパーから筆者への手紙には、筑波山神社の護摩へのお礼とともに、「今日は気分が良く、効いているようだ、必ず生還して日本へ行くから……」とあった。今でもこれを見ると胸が熱くなる。

Charm to him and that "Today I feel very well, the charm seems to be working, I will definitely survive and go to Japan." Even today, when I re-read this letter, I cannot but become shaken.

第8話

素心──ものの本質を見極める心

　モーゼ第4の戒めは"Remember the Sabbath Day, to Keep it Holy（安息日を忘れずに聖なる日とせよ）"である。6日間働き、7日目は安息日として、自らはもちろん、家族、使用人他すべてを安息させよ、という。太陽暦では、ユダヤ人にとっての安息日は土曜日であるが、キリスト教徒にとっては日曜日である。元々エジプトの奴隷であった自分たちを救ってくれた"ユダヤの神（Lord the God）"に感謝をこめて祭祀（神との交流）を行う安息日を守るよう、モーゼは戒めとしたのである。安息日を"忘れずに(remember)"、そして"守る(guard)"という2つのステップをもって3千年余にわたり実践してきたのである。

　ご存知のように、アカデミアにはサバテカル・リーブがある。6年間研究を続けると、7年目に有給休暇を半年から1年与えられ、リフレッシュを兼ねて別の研究室で新しい体験をする。つい最近も、オーストラリアの友人からサバテカル・リーブでオックスフォード大学に来ているという連絡があった。

　さて聖なる安息日といっても、1日中シナゴグ（ユダヤ会堂）やキリスト教会で祈りを捧げるわけではない。リフレッシュした頭で何を考えるかが、有効な時間の使い方というものである。現フォレストラボ（Forest Laboratories）社長兼COOのL. オラノフ氏（L. Olanoff）は、アップジョ

The Eighth Narrative

Possess the Ability to Identify the True Nature of Any Given Thing

Moses' Fourth Commandment of "Remember the Sabbath Day, to Keep it Holy" expresses the practice of working for six days and on the seventh day, rest. Honoring the day of rest was not only for the individual, but for the entire family, as well as related servants and those employed. According to the solar calendar, for the Jewish people, the day of rest or Sabbath is Saturday, and for those of the Christian faith, it is Sunday. It was the intention of Moses to establish this lesson, as a day to express gratitude to the Lord, the God who had saved them from slavery in Egypt, through participating in a spiritual dialogue with God. There are two important words in this Commandment: 'remember" is to ensure that this lesson is not forgotten or neglected, and 'keep' is to guard the tradition. Thus, the true nature of these words has been taken to heart as this Commandment has been sustained for over 3,000 years.

As many of you know, those in academia have what is referred to as a Sabbatical leave. An individual who has conducted research for 6 straight years is allowed on the 7th year a six-month to a one-year paid vacation, providing a 'refresh' period to go into a different research lab for new experiences. Just recently, I received word from a friend in Australia saying that he is on Sabbatical leave and is currently at Oxford University.

Although it's a holy day of rest, or Sabbath, this doesn't imply that the entire day is spent praying in a synagogue, or in the case of the Christians, in a church. It is good time spent to refresh one's mind for renewed beneficial use. The current president and COO of Forest Laboratories, Dr. L. Olanoff, dur-

ン社の研開担当副社長（R&DVP）であった当時、土曜日の会議には一切出ずにシナゴグに行き、後は家でじっくりと次の戦略を練るのが常であった。夫人が陶芸家で、エスニック料理をよくいただいた。また、現イーライリリーCEO、会長兼社長であるキリスト・プロテスタントであるジョン・レックライター氏（John Lechleiter）とは、COO時代に日曜日を一緒に過ごしたことがある。午前、彼の森を2時間ほど歩き、屋根つきの暖炉で話をし（普段は資料を読むという）、家族と共にプロテスタント教会に行って祈り、その後は、やはりゆっくりしていた。彼は、早寝早起きで早朝を有効に使っていた。

"素心"という言葉がある。中国は唐代の書家、顔真卿（がんしんけい）（709～785年）が初めて使った言葉で"平常心でものの本質を見極める心"だという。この素心という言葉を宗教家である友人から、アップジョン（日本法人）の社長になった時に教えられた。

"本質を見極める心"という意味で忘れられない人がいる。当代随一の論客である三菱総合研究所理事長・前東京大学総長の小宮山宏氏である。総長時代（2005～2009年）は"時代の先頭に立つ""他人を感じる心"そして"知の構造化"を説いた。筆者はこの"先頭に立つ"という勇気を思い出して、決心することがよくある。前

唐代の書家・顔真卿

ing his days at Upjohn as VP for R&D, would never attend meetings that were held on Saturdays, but would make it a routine to visit the synagogue, and later spend time with his family, followed by spending a long time thinking about the next strategy to take. His wife was a ceramic artist, and there were many times I enjoyed her ethnic cooking. Further, I had the opportunity to spend a Sunday with Dr. John Lechleiter, the current president, chairman and CEO of Eli Lilly, when he was COO of Lilly. In the morning he would walk in the woods for about 2 hours. If someone joined him on the walk, they would talk by a roofed fireplace. If he was alone he would usually read material. He followed this by a visit to the Protestant church with his family, and later took the rest of the day to relax. He was an early-riser and early-sleeper, and used the early morning hours effectively.

There is a phrase [So-Shin] which is said to have been first used by Tang period chirographer, Gang Shin Kei (709~785), who wrote "With a Calm State of Mind, Possess the Ability to Identify the True Nature of Any Given Thing". I learned this phrase [So-Shin] from a friend, who a person of religion, when I became president of Upjohn Japan.

There is one person I will never forget when remembering the concept of "Possess the Ability to Identify the True Nature of Any Given Thing", and that is Dr. Hiroshi Komiyama, chairman Mitsubishi Research Institute and former president of the University of Tokyo, one of the greatest debaters known in Japan. During his years (2005~2009) as chancellor, he introduced and defined principles such as; "Stand at the Forefront of the Period", "Have the Spirit to Understand Another's Feelings" and "the Structuration of Knowledge". I frequently benefit from the phrase "Stand at the Forefront" because it reminds me to have the courage necessary in making decisions. I had the opportunity to discuss with former president Komiyama the book entitled "The Israel Lobby and U.S. Foreign Policy," which was written by J.J. Mearsheimer and S.M. Walt. Dr. Mearsheimer has in-depth understanding of United States President Obama's Middle East Policy., How this matter will proceed depends on how President Obama will exercise former president

総長とは、今日のオバマ大統領の中東政策にも通ずるJ.J. Mearsheimer & S.M. Waltによる著書'The Israel Lobby and US Foreign Policy'について話が弾んだ。オバマ大統領がどのように前総長のいう"他人を感じる心"を発揮するかである。前総長のスピード感の凄さは濱田純一現総長がジョークで言った"動け東大、動くな小宮山"という言葉が如実に物語っている。

2010年、文化功労者になられた松尾壽之元宮崎医科大学学長は、"ものの本質を見極める心"でコロンブスの卵を実現した。熱により不活化される酵素の本質を応用したのである。生体サンプルを瞬時加熱することにより、必要量のペプチドを確保して、ヒト心房由来の利尿ホルモンである心房利尿ペプチド（ANP）をはじめ、多くの生体ペプチドの同定と合成を成し遂げたのだ。先生はノーベル賞候補の1人でもある。

E.J.コーリー教授（ハーバード大）とJ.レックライター博士（AIMECS-2011にて）

Komiyama's principle of "Have the Spirit to Understand Another's Feelings". Former president Komiyama's sense of speed is legendary. This is vividly reflected in a joke that was made by the current president of the University of Tokyo, Dr. Junichi Hamada, "Move on Tokyo University, Don't move Komiyama".

In 2010, Dr. Toshiyuki Matsuo, former president of the Miyazaki Medical University, recipient of the Persons of Cultural Merit award, and a candidate for the Nobel Prize, through "Possessing the Ability to Identify the True Nature of Any Given Thing," realized Columbus's Egg, which refers to a brilliant discovery that seems simple after the fact. He accomplished this by identifying the true nature of heat inactivated enzymes, and thus was able to retrieve the necessary amount of peptide through heating a biological sample for a short period of time. Beginning with human atrial natriuretic peptide (ANP), he succeeded in identifying and combining numerous biological samples. Each of these examples shows the benefits of possessing the ability to identify the true nature of any given thing, and how successful individuals structure their lives to enhance this ability.

第9話

An independent thinker

　この"An independent thinker（物真似でなく自身で考える）"という言葉は芸術家にとっては当たり前のことかもしれないが、大学院時代の指導教官であったW.L.F.アルマレゴ博士（W.L.F. Armarego）から3年間叩き込まれた教えである。まだ30代半ばだった氏は、ジョン・コーンフォース卿（Sir John Cornforth: オックスフォード大学、1975年ノーベル化学賞受賞）研究室でのサバテカル・リーブから帰ったばかりの1967年、午後のティータイムで、ミルクティーとビスケットを手に持ったまま、熱っぽく「ノーベル賞を目指して仕事をしなくては駄目だ」と語っていた。その姿は今でも鮮やかに蘇る。An independent thinkerであるからこそ、"ものの本質を見極める（参照：第1章第8話）"ことができるのである。

　An independent thinkerが基本のパートナーズ・リーダーシップ社（Partners In Leadership）のイーライリリー研修で得た4ステップ思考は今でもよく活用している。すなわち、課題を与えられた時は、まず"状況を分析し（See it）"、それを"自ら咀嚼し（Own it）"、"解決策を独自に見つけ（Solve it）"、"果敢に実行に移す（Do it）"。1度試してみることをおすすめしたい。目から鱗の体験をすることがある。

　2010年から2011年にかけて、米国研究製薬工業協会（PhRMA Washington DC）関係の米欧の大手製薬企業のCEOが大幅に交代した。

The Ninth Narrative
An Independent Thinker

The phrase 'An independent thinker' may be naturally associated with artists. However, Dr. W.L.F. Armarego, my graduate supervisor during my university days, drilled this phrase into me over the span of three years. Although in his mid-30s, in 1967, he had just returned from a Sabbatical research leave-of-absence in the laboratory of Sir John Cornforth (Oxford University, winner of the 1975 Nobel Prize in Chemistry). I can still vividly remember him at afternoon tea, while having biscuits and hot milk tea, he would passionately say "You have to work as though you are striving for the Nobel Prize". It is only from being 'An Independent Thinker' that an individual can 'Possess the Ability to Identify the True Nature of Any Given Thing.' (Refer to Narrative No. 8)

The concept of 'An independent thinker' is the fundamental principle within Eli Lilly and Company's "Partners In Leadership" program, which is structured from four steps that I absorbed during my years at the firm and frequently utilize even today. In short, when an issue arises, it is vital to 1. 'See it' (analyze the circumstance); 2. 'Own it' (ruminate or take the initiative for the issue); 3. 'Solve it' (find a solution); and finally 4. 'Do it' (boldly proceed to act upon it). Allow me to suggest that everyone try this concept at least once. You may experience a true eye opener.

From last year to this year, there were significant changes to the CEOs of major U.S. and European pharmaceutical companies that belong to the Pharmaceutical Research and Manufacturers Association (PhRMA, Washington DC). Compared to the time when an MBA was the norm, now the CEOs

かつてのMBA全盛時代からR&D、弁護士、経済学、公認会計士、セールスと多様な経験を有し、An independent thinkerであるエキスパートがCEOとなっている。しかも垂直統合から水平統合となりCEO自らが決断をする体制となってきた。この水平統合の下、ビジネスユニット、人事、戦略、R&Dなど横並びとして自ら運営しなくてはならない部門を除いて、いかにアウトソーシングできるかが生き残りの分岐点である。いずれ米欧の大手もホールディング化する傾向にある。

　各企業の戦略は急激で、オーソライズド後発品戦略、バイオベター戦略（バイオ後続品）等々、協会が追い付いていけない程のスピードである。例えば、先発メーカーの集団であるPhRMA（米国研究製薬工業協会）などは、先発メーカーの利益を目指して活動してきた。企業間の合従連携は、新薬をめぐるものだけでなく、販路をめぐってもますます盛んになり、企業間の再編も盛んであるが、BIO（米国のバイオテクノロジー産業協会）による最近の"21st Century FDA（21世紀のFDA）"などをみると、協会の再編も視野に入ってきたのかなという感じがする。日本も然りである。

　最初に触れたAn independent thinkerたる芸術家を紙上で知る機会を得た。英国における最高の文学賞マン・ブッカー賞（Man Booker Prize）の国際賞であるマン・ブッカー国際賞（Man Booker International Prize）を2011年5月19日に受賞した米国のフィリップ・ミルトン・ロス（Philip Milton Roth）である。氏はユダヤ系移民の子として1933年に生まれ、9歳の時に両親とともにコネチカット州のニューアークの田園に移り住んだ。ゴイム（Goyim、ユダヤにとっての異教徒）の中での体験を時間をかけて検証し、執筆するという。第2次世界大戦中のニューアークにおけるポリオ感染の出来事を書いたのは2010年であった（'Nemesis'：天

represent a variety of backgrounds, including scientists, attorneys, economists, CPAs, and sales professionals. They are a new breed of experts and independent thinkers. In addition, an organization structural shift from vertical integration to horizontal integration is occurring. Under horizontal integration, the CEO personally makes decisions, and divisions such as the business units, human resources (personnel), strategy, and R&D are lined up, while divisions that must be operated independently are excluded. Determining just what can be out-sourced is a key to survival. This has led to the trend of major U.S. and European pharmaceutical companies becoming holding companies.

Individual company's strategies are extremely complex and can change rapidly. They include authorized generic product strategies, biosimilar strategies, and many others. The speed is too fast for PhRMA to keep pace. For example, PhRMA is an association formed by a group of innovative research-based pharmaceutical manufacturers; it is for the benefit of these manufacturers that PhRMA was initiated. However, as the competition increasingly becomes more active, this joint coalition of companies is not merely competing with each other in the areas of new drugs, sales channels, and other matters. Active corporate restructuring is taking place, and according to the U.S.'s Biotechnology Industry Organization (BIO), in a recent article (Can a 21st Century FDA Accelerate Biotech Innovation to Cure Disease and Save Lives? Sept 29, 2011), it looks as though they have their sights on restructuring the FDA as well. Japan should be thinking in the same way.

Going back to the initially mentioned 'An independent thinker', I had an opportunity to get to know an artist who was an author. It is American author Philip Milton Roth, who on May 19, 2011, won the Man Booker International Prize, one of the highest literary prizes, which is given to a living author of any nationality for a body of work. Mr. Roth was born to Jewish immigrants in 1933, and at age nine, with his parents, moved to rural Newark, Connecticut. He wrote about the experience of living among Gyoim (those who are non-Jewish), and took a great deal of time to document this within his book. In 2010 he wrote the 'Nemesis' in which he writes of the

罰)。氏は他に多くの賞を、例えば2001年には第1回フランツ・カフカ賞を受賞している。ある人曰く「仮にもう1つの国際賞(おわかりと思う)をもらったとしても、すでに巨匠であることに変わりはない」。

W.L.F. アルマレゴ博士と(2009年)

1967年からの友人ピーター・グリーン博士と(2012年)

outbreak of polio in Newark during World War II. Mr. Roth has been the recipient of many prizes and awards; for instance, in 2001 he received the first Franz Kafka Prize. According to a certain individual, "Even if he received one more international literary prize (I think you will know which), the fact that he is a master author will not change."

Independent thinkers are found in many professions including research scientists in academia, CEOs of major pharmaceutical companies, leaders of major trade organizations, and artists. They 'Possess the Ability to Identify the True Nature of Any Given Thing' which helps them be successful in their endeavors.

第10話
「余人をもって代えがたい」はない

　1966年11月23日、日米衛星放送が開始され、画面に飛び込んで来たのは、J.F. ケネディ大統領の暗殺と、L.B. ジョンソン副大統領が第36代大統領としてエアフォース・ワン機内で女性連邦判事に宣誓する映像であった。一時的混乱と対ベトナム政策への影響はあったが、米国が沈没することはなかった。あのケネディでさえ、亡くなれば新しい体制が生まれるのだ。

　筆者は、自らの体験から"余人を以って代えがたい"ということはないと学んだ。1970年からほぼ40年、米国との関わりの中で、4回の転職を体験することになったが、1回を除いて自らの意思でやめたことはなく、やめる環境が自然と整うという不思議なめぐり合わせとなった。ここで、自らに代わる人はいくらでもいることを自覚するとともに、次の戦いである敗者復活戦を勝ち抜くため、常日頃から自らの"天命 (mission)"を自覚して時の組織に貢献することを学んだ。誠心誠意努力する人を天は見捨てないものである。

　"余人を以って代えがたい"人物の例外がいる。中国における毛沢東主席である。最近、特に毛思想への回帰の傾向が見られる。それは、前述の裏返しである。現体制を変えたくないからである。中国は急に変われない国なのである。しかし、医療関係の充実は急速に進む。社会保障・

The Tenth Narrative

Anyone is Expendable

On the 23rd of November, 1963 the first satellite broadcast between Japan and the United States was that of the assignation of President J.F. Kennedy. It was followed by the swearing in of Vice President L.B. Johnson as the 36th President aboard Air Force One by a female federal judge. Although there was a short period of turmoil and impact in its Vietnam policy, the United States did not sink. Even with someone as important as President Kennedy, when an era ends, a new system is born.

I, through experience, have learned that anyone is expendable. Since 1970, for almost 40 years, I have been involved with the U.S., during which I have changed jobs four times. Within those four changes, it was only once that I had taken the initiative to change. It is strange how things fall into place to form an environment that induces someone to quit a job. It is then that the realization sets in that you are expendable, and that you must prepare yourself for the next battle, to continue to win the consolation matches. I have learned to always be conscious of my mission, and contribute to the organization that I am member of at the time. Heaven does not forsake one who strives with the best of intentions.

There is one person who is an exception to being expendable. He is China's Chairman Mao Zedong. Recently, there has been a return to Maoism in China. This trend reflects the opposite of what I had previously written. China is a nation that cannot change quickly because they do not want to change the current system. However, there has been rapid progress in implementing changes to their health care and medical sector. Social security and

医療はそもそも社会主義的な性格のものであるからだ。

　民主主義社会にも、時間限定で考えると余人を以って代えがたい人物は存在する。条件は何か。"進む時は人に押され、退く時は自ら決す"ことができる人である。世間も政治家も政府も大賛成だったのに、首相になることを固辞した伊東正義氏のような人である（1989年）。

　アップジョン時代のCEOであったDr. クーパーについては何度か触れた（参照：第1章第1・7話）が、時代の流れを察し、アップジョン・ファミリー以外で最初のCEOとしてDr.クーパーを任命したテッド・パーフィットCEO（Ted Parfet）について述べたい。氏は筆者がアップジョンに入社した時のCEOであった。パーフィット氏は、第2代社長W. E.アップジョンの孫娘と結婚して、ファミリー入りした。いつも笑みを絶やさず、ワイシャツ姿（in shirt sleeves）で仕事をする人であった。第2次大戦中はB-25のパイロットとしてイタリア・オーストリア戦線におり、帰国後ミシガン大学で財務を学んだ。アップジョンに入り頭角を現して孫娘と結婚されたというだけあって、穏やかで品格のある方であった。

　氏の凄いところは、すでに1989年にこれからの医薬品企業がR&D投資を積極的に行う必要がある環境になることを考え、ファミリーとは関係のない元厚生教育省次官・コーネル大学医学部長であるDr. クーパーを後継者に選んだことである。氏のビジネススタイルは、コンセンサスが基本であったが、自ら決めなくてはならない時は恐れなかった。それではなぜコンセンサスなのか。曰く「コンセンサスだと支持する人がそれだけ多くなり、決定とその結果がそれだけ良いものになるという自らの体験があったからだ」。

health care (e.g., Medicare and Medicaid in the U.S.) possess the characteristics of socialism.

Even within a democratic society, although limiting the time period under consideration, one could ask whether there was ever an individual who was un-expendable. What would the conditions be that would make this so? An individual who possessed the principle "To proceed with the backing of all, to retreat on one's decision" could be such an un-expendable person. An individual who had the support of the public, politicians and bureaucrats, and yet chose not to become the Prime Minister of Japan was Mr. Masayoshi Itoh (1989).

I have written numerous times (refer to Narratives 1 & 7) of Dr. Cooper, who I was fortunate to have known during my days at Upjohn. He was the first CEO to be appointed outside of the Upjohn family. Former CEO Ted Parfet appointed Dr. Cooper through his perception of the changes that were to come to the pharmaceutical industry. I would like to write about my experience with Mr. Parfet, who was the CEO when I joined the Company. He was a member of the Upjohn family through marriage to the granddaughter of the second president Dr. W. E. Upjohn. I remember Mr. Parfet as a man who always had a smile on his face and worked in his shirt sleeves. During the Second World War he flew missions to the front lines over Italy and Australia as a B-25 pilot. After returning to the U.S., he went to the University of Michigan and majored in finance. He joined Upjohn, and immediately distinguished himself at work. I will remember him for his gentle and graceful manner.

What really impresses me about Mr. Parfet is, in 1989, he had the foresight to perceive that the environment was going to call for pharmaceutical companies to actively make investments in R&D. He selected as his successor an individual who had no ties with the Upjohn family, and who was a former Under Secretary of Welfare, and former head of the medical department of Cornell University, Dr. Cooper. Mr. Parfet's business style was based on consensus; however, he was never afraid of making his own decisions. Then what

最近の流れとしては、1980年代とは違って、コンセンサスに時間をかけている余裕がない時代になったのもまた事実である。生き馬の目を抜くスピードが求められているのが現状である。

is consensus? He said, "If it is decided through consensus, resulting in many people supporting the idea or plan, which means that the decision and the results are all the more better.' This was probably learned through his own experience.

Recent trends, differing from that of the 1980s, reflect that the luxury of taking the time to get a consensus is over. Today's reality is that speed is required to be competitive.

Mr.Ted Perfet.Jr (1987)
A CENTURY OF CARING, Upjohn

第11話
敬愛するも従属せず

　モーゼ第5の戒めは、"Honor Your Father and Your Mother.（あなたの父上や母上を敬愛せよ）"である。ここで言う"Your Father and Your Mother"とは、両親、長老、賢人と言われる人々である。子供にとっての学校の先生なども考えられる。また"Honor（敬愛）"と"Obey（従属）"は違うという。自らの両親を敬愛しても、従属を意味するものではないということである。本章第9話の"An independent thinker（物真似でなく自身で考える）"に通じる言葉でもある。成人し、自らの人生の決断をする時、両親の意にそぐわなくても、親切心を以って両親を敬うことである。しかし、ユダヤの律に反する決断は許されない。ここがモーゼらしいところである。

　ここで忘れられないのは、『「謝ってすむ問題じゃない！」で、どうする？』（ベストセラーズ、2004年）の著者である米川耕一弁護士である。20年余りの御交誼をいただいている。氏は東京大学文学部心理学科在学中に司法試験に合格した弁護士にして臨床心理学者でもある異才の方である。

　氏の基本精神は、"愛"である。職業柄、多種多様な人々や事件に遭遇しているに違いないが、常に氏の言う"愛"を以って事に当たっている。私などは、よく事に当たって勝ちに行く姿勢を戒められている。勝って

The Eleventh Narrative

To Honor but Not to Obey

"Honor Your Father and Your Mother" is the Fifth Commandment of Moses. Although "Your Father and Your Mother" is noted, in a broader perspective, it is directed to include, of course, your parents, as well as your elders, and those who possess wisdom, such as philosophers, teachers, etc. For a child, it may be a teacher. Also, to honor and to obey differ. You may certainly honor your parents, but that does not mean that you obey them. It may be similar to the concept of 'an independent thinker', which was touched upon in the ninth narrative. Upon reaching adulthood and making decisions in your own life that may differ from your parent's expectations, you must sustain kindness and love toward your parents. However, within the Jewish Faith, decisions that go against the Jewish rules are forbidden. It is very much like the way Moses led the Israelites in not tolerating violations of the laws.

At this point, there is someone I cannot forget who is bestselling author of "It's not something you can apologize for! Then what is there to do?", and attorney, Mr. Koichi Yonekawa. For almost 20 years I have had the great pleasure of being acquainted with him. Mr. Yonekawa, during his studies in both the Department of Literature and the Psychology Department at the University of Tokyo, had taken and passed his bar exams to become an attorney of law, as well as a becoming a clinical psychotherapist. He is truly a man of exceptional talent and knowledge.

His fundamental principle is 'Love'. By profession, it is highly predictable that he would come in contact with a wide variety of people, as well as incidents. He always says that it is with a sense of 'Love' with which he ap-

何が残るのか、愛(相互の理解と敬愛)が生まれなければ価値のある勝負ではなく、時間とエネルギーの無駄ということである。

　また米川夫人の千鶴様もスーパーパワーの持ち主で、フランス文化に詳しく、両御両親をたいそう"敬愛(Honor)"しているが、"従属(Obey)"ではない(と思う)。夫人の社交ダンスの発表会では、年に一度の別世界を家内ともども満喫させていただいている。クリスマス時の米川夫妻とのフレンチ会食は毎年店を変え、時を忘れて談論風発、スーパーパワーによる来る年の予言に耳を傾ける至福の時でもある。そのような中で学んだのは、とてつもない偶然と思っていた出来事が根拠のある必然で起きていることに気づくようになったことである。

　最近親しくなったシリコンバレーのベンチャーアルデリックス(ARDELYX)のCEOであるマイク・ラーブ氏(Mike Raab)も両親を敬愛してやまない人である。その名前から、カーク・ラーブ氏(Kirk Raab)と関係があるのかと問うと、息子だという。カーク・ラーブ氏とは彼が米国アボット社(Abbott)の社長だった頃、よく交渉事をした間柄だった。後ジネンテック(Genentech)のCEOとなり一時代を築いたベンチャーのチャンピオンだった人である。奇遇に驚くと同時に、瞬時に両親の良い所を受け継いだ好漢であることが判った。

　彼の基本も"愛"である。両親を"敬愛(Honor)"し、特に菜食主義者の母親に対する敬愛は深く、納豆、豆腐から小豆と日本名で話し、納豆が好物という。

　"アンチ・レピンスキー(Anti-Lipinski)"法則が、その科学技術の基本である。すなわち、普通なら医薬品をいかにして体内に吸収させるか

proaches each task. I, on the other hand, have the tendency to approach each task with a competitive mind set, and thus try frequently to correct this attitude. What remains from just winning? Without love (mutual understanding and honor), there is no value in the competition, resulting in a waste of time and energy.

I must add that his wife, Chizuru, also possesses exceptional energy and talent, with an outstanding understanding of French literature. She honors, but I believe does not obey, both of her parents greatly. I enter a totally different world when attending Mrs. Yonekawa's annual social dancing exhibition with my wife, an event we both thoroughly enjoy. Every Christmas, at a different French restaurant, we have the great pleasure of engaging in conversations involving a variety of topics with the Yonekawa's. This provides me with the added opportunity and benefit of absorbing what these two powerful people predict for the coming year. What I have come to realize through these engagements is that events that I had originally perceived as unbelievably coincidental, were in fact meant to occur.

Recently I had the opportunity to become acquainted with Mike Raab, CEO of the venture firm ARDELYX, who evidently honors both parents enormously. From his surname, I enquired upon his relationship with Kirk Raab, to which he responded is his father. I had the chance to interact with Mr. Kirk Raab when he was the president of Abbott of the U.S. Later he became a champion of the age for venture capital firms through his tenure as CEO of Genentech. Simultaneously surprised by the coincidence, I immediately concluded that Mike had inherited the superior aspects of both his parents.

Mike's fundamental principle is 'Love' as well. It is evident that he honors his parents, and toward his mother, who is vegetarian, it is particularly deep. Speaking with him, he will mention 'tofu', 'natto' (fermented soy beans), and 'azuki' (red beans) by their Japanese names. He has said that he is especially fond of 'natto'.

The basic principle of "Anti-Lipinski" is scientific technology. Meaning,

に腐心するのに、腸より吸収させない事で治療を目指すという。逆転の発想の創薬ベンチャーで、臨床フェーズⅡbに入っている化合物もある。治療域も慢性腎不全から利尿、糖尿と応用範囲が拡大している。

　執行役員会も、皆率直に意見を出し、最後はサッサッと各自のメトリックスを決めて終了。昼食も社員と一緒に同じものをいただく。ベンチャーらしくとても良い雰囲気の会社である。成功を祈ってやまない。

conventionally researchers at ARDELYX develop drugs that target proteins found in the gut whose activities affect the entire body. They also examine how the body absorbs a specific drug, but then strive toward a treatment that would be accomplished by avoiding the absorption from occurring in the intestinal tract. Drugs that are not absorbed can achieve systemic efficacy while avoiding systemic toxicity and side effects. It is common for a drug development venture to conduct reverse-method approaches, and a number of chemical compounds are in clinical phase II stages. The areas of treatment and application range have expanded into chronic kidney failure, diuresis, and diabetes.

At ARDELYX operating meetings, frank and candid comments are made, individual matrixes are established and meetings are concluded swiftly. During lunch, executive management is often seen eating with employees. The company has a good atmosphere, that of a venture. I cannot help but pray for their success.

第12話
人(他人・部下)を故意に殺めてはいけない

　モーゼ第6の戒めは、"You shall not murder.（故意に人を殺めてはいけない）"である。この戒めは"You shall not kill."と誤解されるという。ユダヤの律では、"人を殺める(murder)"と"殺める(killing)"は、明らかに違う。murderは故意にヒトを殺めることであり、法的にも許されない。killingは、法的にも認められる範囲で殺めることである。正当防衛か、戦争の時などである。

　人文科学や自然科学のグローバルスタンダーズに基づく場合は別であるが、その評価基準が明確でない環境における人事では、往々にして不当に人が排除された例を見てきた。これは、社会的なmurderである。

　最近、経済産業省を退職した古賀茂明氏が、もし米国の官僚であったらどうするだろうか、とだいぶ前に考えたことがあった。とうの昔に官僚を辞して、民主党系であれ、共和党系であれ、名の通ったシンクタンクに移ったであろうということは、想像に難くない。そこが、米国の良いところで、議員にロビーをかけて、自分の改革案を織り込んだ議員立法を成し遂げていたかもしれない。このような人財をmurderしてはいけない。生かしてこそ、人財である。

　海外にもっと生々しく興味深い人物がいる。murderとkillingの両方

The Twelfth Narrative
Do Not Deliberately Kill

The Sixth Commandment of Moses is "You shall not murder". It is said that this Commandment is misunderstood and translated as "You shall not kill". In Jewish teachings, there is a significant difference between 'murder' and 'kill'. Murder is the deliberate act of killing another individual and is by law unforgiveable. Killing, in some circumstances such as self-defense and war, is accepted under the law.

Not including the basis for the global standards of humanities and natural science, in an environment that lacks an evaluation code, there are a number of cases in personnel management where an individual faces unjustified elimination. This in its own way is murder.

Some time ago, I thought about what would have happened if Mr. Shigeaki Koga, recently resigned from the Ministry of Economy, Trade and Industry (METI), had been a bureaucrat in the United States. It was not difficult to imagine that he would have left his job with the government, and become a member of a prestigious democratic- or republican-related think-tank. This is what is good about America. He could have been lobbying with members of congress, which would have perhaps led to the inclusion of his positions or proposals into congressional legislation. It is not right to allow the murder of a human resource of this caliber. It is only through allowing the human resource to fulfill its potential, does it become a resource.

Looking abroad, there are individuals who are vivid and profound individuals. One such individual would be Mr. Dominique Strauss-Kahn, former IMF managing director, who is experiencing both aspects of 'murder' and

を体験しつつある前IMF専務であったドミニク・ストラウス－カーン氏（Dominique Strauss-Kahn、フランス）である。2012年のフランス大統領選では、ニコラス・サルコジ元大統領（Nicolas Sarkozy）に対する左派候補者として有力視されていた人物である。元々、彼の女性に対する異常性には注目が集まっていた。

　一般論であるが、日本独特の潔癖性と違って、欧米では女性スキャンダルに関して一寸感覚的に違うところがある。クリントン大統領（Clinton）のモニカ（Monica）事件、ミッテラン大統領（Mitteran）の婚外子、サルコジ大統領（Sarkozy）の離婚歴などの捉え方に、それが男性としての魅力であるかのような感性があり、女性票が入るのである。イタリアのベルルスコーニ首相（Berlusconi）は別として。

　ドミニク・ストラウス－カーン氏に話を戻そう。まずモーゼの律ではmurderと判断できそうなニューヨークでの事件についてである。彼は滞在先のホテルのメイドであるN.Dディアロ（Ms.N.Diallo）に対して性的攻撃をしたという訴えを受けて、検察当局は74年間の服役という量刑に言及していた。もちろんストラウス－カーン側にも腕利きの弁護士、ベンジャミン・ブラフマン（Benjamin Brafman）がつき、調査により、N.ディアロが麻薬取引や、マネーロンダリングに絡む女性であるという事を示した。検察もN.ディアロの訴えの信憑性を疑い、400万ドルの保証金を拒否されていたストラウス－カーン氏は保釈されたのである。その裁判にあたったニューヨーク地方検事サイラス・ヴァンス氏（Cyrus Vance）が、元国務長官ヴァンス氏（Vance）の息子であるということでも話題を呼んだ。一連のスキャンダルは誰が仕組んだmurderだったのか。この件に関して、ストラウス－カーンは正義（justice）を勝ち取った。

'killling'. In 2012, he was seen as a strong left-wing contender against the then incumbent French President Nicolas Sarkozy. There was also accumulating attention focused on his aggressive actions toward women.

Although it is common belief that Japanese have their particular sense of morality, there is definitely a difference in how they perceive matters compared to America. For example, in the cases of U.S. President Clinton and Monica Lewinsky, French President Mitteraand's child out of wedlock, and the divorce record of former French President Sarkozy, the behaviors of those involved were viewed as positive male attributes and resulted in an increased number of women's votes. However, this was not the case for Italian Prime Minister Berlusconi.

Let me return to Mr. Dominique Strauss-Kahn. Moses' teaching regarding 'murder' can be seen in the incident in New York. It was in this city that he was charged with sexually assaulting Ms. N. Diallo, a maid at the hotel where he as staying at the time. The district attorney was going to prosecute him and pursue a sentence of 74 years in prison. Needless to say, Strauss-Kahn's side employed an extremely capable lawyer, Benjamin Brafman, and through their investigation into Ms. N. Diallo, found that she was involved in drugs and money laundering. The prosecution was also having doubts of Ms. N. Diallo, and allowed certain evidence to be admitted into the trial. Mr. Strauss-Kahn was allowed to pay the bail of $4million and was released. A topic of conversation was that the New York District Prosecutor was Mr. Cyrus Vance, the son of former Secretary of State Vance. Was this public 'murder' the result of a conspiracy? Whatever the backdrop, as far as this incident is concerned, it seems that he was able to obtain justice.

Next I would like to look into if there was any sort of validity in the 'killing' of the same individual. On September 1, Mr. Strauss-Kahn left New York to return to Paris. However, for several months, a preliminary investigation involving his sexual assault toward Ms. Tristane Banon, an author, was already underway. This assault, with its many dark elements, was reported to have taken place in 2003. However, her mother had decided to keep the incident

次に、同一人物に対するkillingは妥当かということである。2011年9月1日、ストラウス–カーン氏はニューヨークを離れ、パリに戻った。しかし、パリでは7月より作家のトリステン・バノン夫人（Ms. Tristane Banon）の訴えによって、氏の性的攻撃に関する予備審査が始まっている。この事件は2003年に起きたが、彼女の母親が国会議員であったため、当時、飛ぶ鳥を落とす勢いだったストラウス–カーン氏が母親に及ぼす影響力を考えて、訴えを起こすことを思いとどめさせたという。ストラウス–カーン氏は2012年の大統領選挙に希望をもって帰国したが、これではとても無理である。この場合、彼はユダヤの律により、killingすべき存在であり、個人的な見解であるが公職追放に値する人物であると思われる。

quiet because she was a member of parliament and, at the time, Mr. Strauss-Kahn was extremely influential. Although he may have had great aspirations toward the then upcoming presidential elections, all probability of this opportunity has now been lost. It is here that perhaps, taking from the Jewish teachings, a 'killing' should take place. In a strictly personal view, I think he should receive a public purging.

第13話

不倫はするな
―― 責任を持てないなら不倫はするな

　モーゼ第7の戒めは、"You shall not commit adultery.（不倫を犯してはならない）"である。ユダヤ社会の旧約聖書の時代には、一夫多妻（polygamy）が認められていた。アラブの世界では今でもそうであるが。一夫多妻の制度はあったが、新婚の夫婦には、新婦を喜ばせるための種々の律法があった。例えば、新郎は新婦と一緒に暮らせるよう1年間の兵役免除があった。家にいて妻を大切にするためである。また夫が転職をしたいと考えても、家からたびたび離れなくてはならない職の場合、妻は夫の転職を拒否することが認められていた。種々の律法により妻達の権利を保護しているのである。これ程までに妻の権利を保護しているのに不倫が取りざたにされる対象は妻のみである。これ程までに法で保護しているから、妻が対象ということなのかもしれない。一夫多妻制度であった当時は、"adulteress（女性の不倫者）"のみが存在していたのである。

　ある時よりヨーロッパのユダヤ社会で一夫多妻制が禁止され、これがユダヤ社会の慣習となった。以来、厳しい律法の下で、一夫一婦制となり、不倫の後の始末も"adulterers（夫）"、"adulteress（妻）"の両者に求められることとなったのである。このように見ていくと、実は旧約聖書の時代でも一般家庭においては、実際のところ一夫一婦制のようなものだったのかもしれないという気がしてくる。

The Thirteenth Narrative

Don't Commit Adultery If You Cannot Take the Responsibility

Moses' Seventh Commandment is "You shall not commit adultery". During the days of the Old Testament, in Jewish society, the practice of polygamy was allowed. In many Arab nations, it is still allowed today. Although polygamy was present, there were a number of laws that were for the benefit of newlywed couples. For example, to ensure that the groom would be able to live with the bride and establish a strong marital foundation, he was given one year of immunity from military service. This allowed the groom to return to his home and take care of his wife. In addition, if the husband decided to make a career change, but as a result would mean that he would be frequently away from home, his wife had the right to reject the career change. It was through these numerous laws that the rights of the wives were being safe-guarded. Even with these abundant safe-guards for the rights of women, when it came to adultery, it was only directed to the wives. It is perhaps because they were so safe-guarded in other ways that adultery pertained only to the wives. During the days when polygamy was practiced, there were only adulteresses existing.

From about 1000 C.E., the Jewish communities in Europe banned the practice of polygamy, and monogamy became a common established practice among the Jewish people. After this point in time, under strict laws, monogamous marriages were established which perhaps made the responsibility of adultery encompass both the husband (adulterer) and wife (adulteress). Looking back, I have the feeling that even during the period of the Old Testament, the average household was probably based upon a monogamous union.

支配階級では強烈な一夫多妻制が見られる。ユダヤ初代王ダビデの息子である第3代ユダヤ王ソロモン（正妻の子ではない）は、エジプトのファラオの娘を娶ったが、エチオピアのシバの女王とのロマンスで有名である。ソロモンが見初めたとも、見初められたとも言われるシバの女王との間に、息子のメネリク1世をもうけている。驚くべきは、3千年もの時を経た1991年に、イスラエル政府により行われた"ソロモン作戦（エチオピアで迫害されているファラシャと呼ばれるユダヤ系エチオピア人1万人を空輸する救出作戦）"のことである。当時、筆者はユダヤの凄さに驚きを禁じ得なかった。

　話を進めよう。この機会にこの第7の戒めがユダヤ社会の何に基づいているのか考えてみたい。それはおそらく、ユダヤの民全員が"ユダヤの子 (the children of Israel)"として1つの大きな家族のメンバーであるということを民族の価値としてきたことにある。ユダヤの律法は、この大きな家族を律するためのものであり、歴史そのものであったのである（前述の1991年ソロモン作戦の動機とも捉え得る）。さらには"個々の家族 (the individual family unit)"を律するために、多くの戒め（全613戒）が経験的に選ばれた。その第7番目に選ばれたのが、"You shall not commit adultery"である。家族の絆と維持を大切にするための戒めである。

　話を現実に戻そう。1980年代の米国ビジネス界で、不倫の末にエグゼクティブが秘書と結婚するケースを見てきた。仕事のできる猛烈な人が多かった。責任をとり、多額の慰謝料を払い、残された妻子の面倒もみている。その後の人生で大成功した人もいるし、要は本人次第ということである。ただ、このような事の起こる会社には何かが欠けていたし、起こらない会社には創業者（創業家）の信念に基づいた伝統・文化というものが根付いていた（参照：第1章第6話）。

The ruling class, we can see, had a very strong tendency to practice polygamy. The first Jewish king, David, had a son (not from his wedded wife)Solomon, who became the third Jewish king. Solomon married the daughter of an Egyptian pharaoh, but his romance with Ethiopian Queen of Sheba is all too famous. Whether it was King Solomon or Queen Sheba who first fell in love with the other is up for debate, however, a son was born between them, Menelik I. What is truly surprising is that almost 3,000 years later, the Jewish people still felt a kinship as seen when the Israeli government embarked upon 'Operation Solomon', which involved an airlift evacuation of some 10,000 Ethiopians Jews who were being persecuted. At the time, I was truly surprised at the scale and lengths to which the Jewish people would go in support of their people.

To continue this narrative, I would like to take the opportunity to look into what principle upon which the Seventh Commandment is based within the Jewish society. It is perhaps based on the concept that all Jewish people are the children of Israel, which would in turn reflect the values of one large family. In the Jewish Torah, the concept of the Jewish people as one large family can be seen throughout their history, (for example, the aforementioned 1991 'Operation Solomon'). In addition, there are many rules (in all 613) within their teachings that have been chosen through experience and are directed toward individual family units. The seventh one to be chosen was "You shall not commit adultery". It is an important rule to ensure that family ties are honored and safe-guarded.

To bring the narrative back to the present, during the 1980s in the American business sector, there were many cases where an executive would marry his secretary. Many were tremendously successful and powerful businessmen. Some would take responsibility and pay large sums in alimony to take care of their wife and children. Later perhaps they would find someone that was important to their lives; it all depended on the individual. In a company where this happens, there must be something missing. However, in a company where this does not occur, it is probably through the continuity of the founder/

最後に、この不倫という題は、なかなか取り上げにくいテーマだと考えたが、モーゼの第7の戒めのお陰で取り上げることができた。モーゼに深謝。

ソロモンとシバの女王

founding family's tradition and culture, which was based upon their convictions. (Refer to narrative No. 6)

Lastly, I thought it would be difficult to write about adultery. However as it was unavoidable to discuss the Seventh Commandment of Moses, I found I was able to address it. I express my gratitude to Moses.

第14話
有形・無形を問わず、盗人になってはならない

　モーゼ第8の戒めは、"You shall not steal.（盗んではならない）"である。旧約聖書時代の"steal"は人を盗むことを意味していた。今日の"誘拐（kidnapping）"である。もちろん、自分の持ち物ではない物を盗むことも禁じられていたが、元々は人浚(ひとさら)い（攫）について言ったのである。ユダヤの律によって物を盗んだことが確定すると、まずそれを返すこと、ケースによっては倍以上にして返すことになる。例えば、牛や羊を1頭盗めば、2頭以上を返すことになる。またそれを殺して肉を売ると、牛は5頭を羊は4頭を返すなど……。当時も、詐欺や、法外な請求、不十分な支払いなどは厳しく罰せられている。有形・無形を問わず、盗んではならないのである。

　"steal"とは、今様に言えば、知的財産をはじめビジネス上の有形・無形を問わず、アイデアを盗むことでもある。最近話題になっている盗聴などは、その典型である。

　ワシントンDCのペンシルバニア通りを下り、湖畔に出て散策すると、必ず目に入ってくるのは、かの有名なウォーターゲート（Watergate）ビルディングである。毎回「ここがね〜」という気持ちになる不思議なところである。日本だったらどうだったろうと思う。国会で、いわゆる代議士と呼ばれる国民の代理人によって選ばれる日本の首相とは違って、共

The Fourteenth Narrative

Innocent or Guilty, Do Not Become a Thief

The Eighth Commandment of Moses is "You shall not steal". During the period of the Old Testament, "to steal" was to steal a human being. Today, we refer to it as kidnapping. Needless to say, to take what does not belong to you is forbidden, but originally the reference was made toward those who abducted people. In the Jewish laws, if it was established that property was indeed stolen, the first step to be taken was to return it. Depending upon the case, there may have been a requirement to multiply the property when returning it. For example, if a head of cattle or sheep was taken, then 2 head of cattle or sheep had to be returned. If the stolen head of cattle or sheep had been slaughtered and sold as meat, then to return this would require 5 head of cattle and 4 head of sheep, and so on. At the time, crimes such as fraud, unlawfully high pricing, and not meeting payment requirements were severely punished by law. For this Commandment, it does not matter whether you are proven innocent or guilty under the Law; you are not to steal.

"Steal" in today's world, may well refer to the theft of intellectual property. In the perspective of businesses, it is not whether individuals are found innocent or guilty under the Law, it is still theft. The recent incidents of wiretapping, as described below, are perfect examples of this.

If you walk down Pennsylvania Avenue in Washington D.C., around the waterfront, you cannot miss the famous Watergate building. Each time I view the building, I am overcome by a strange feeling when I reflect on what occurred within this complex. Again, I cannot help wondering what if it had happened in Japan. Representatives of the Diet, who are said to be represent-

和制で国民によって直接（少し違うが）選ばれる米国の大統領には、間に入って調整してくれる人（代議士達）はいない。間違っていれば、自ら責任を取る事になる。例えばニクソン大統領は弾劾裁判の前に決断をした。今ではその業績が再評価されつつあるが。

　最近の話題としては、ニュースコープ（News Corp）のCEOであるルパート・マードック氏（Rupert Murdoch）がニュース・インターナショナル（News International、氏のロンドン拠点の子会社、CEOレベッカ・ブルックス女史［Ms. Rebekah Brooks］は現在は退任）を介して行った盗聴事件が有名である。盗聴の対象が上流階級、政治家、そして王室関係者（とくれば、思い出すことがある？）のボイスメールときては、厄介である。168年の歴史を誇るタブロイド誌NOW（News of the World）が廃刊に追い込まれた。ルパート・マードックは筆者がオーストラリア国立大学大学院に在籍の頃（1970年）から、長年憧れに似た気持ちで眺め、注目してきた人物であるだけに、ここまでやっていたのかという思いがある。氏は、オーストラリア出身ながら、若くしてロンドンのTimesを買収し、世界のメディア王を目指し始めていた。その後米国にも進出し、最近Wall Street Journalを買収し、まさに世界制覇を成し遂げた矢先である。歴代のイギリス首相が恐れ、そしてご機嫌もとってきた怪物であるが、今回の事件では、キャメロン首相（Cameron）がロンドン警視庁に捜査命令を出した。高齢の氏が、後継を長男のジェームス（James）に移すために無数の子会社の再編に入った矢先の出来事だった。しかし、氏はしたたかで、ニュース・インターナショナル（News International）のCEOになると表明している。筆者若き日の憧れでもあったマードック（Murdoch）が"天罰（nemeisis）"を受けるのか注目である。

　ところで、本章第3話で"エグゼクティブ・パイプライン（Exective

ing the people, elect the Prime Minister of Japan. This differs from the democratic process of which the people (although slightly different) directly vote for the President of the United States. This system does not have the people who are in between the voters and the president and do the coordination work ? i.e., a member of the Diet. If a mistake occurs, they take the responsibility. President Nixon, prior to his possible impeachment trial, made his decision and was forced to take the responsibility. Now, there is a move to re-evaluate his accomplishments and contributions.

A more recent incident of wiretapping involves News International, which is based in London and owned by News Corp.'s CEO Mr. Rupert Murdoch. Through News International's CEO Ms. Rebekah Brooks (resigned), the Company had conducted phone-hacking, which is now notoriously famous. The phone-hacking targets were members of high society, actors, MPs, and even the Royal Household (reminds me of someone). Listening in on voice mail, can mean trouble. As a result, the tabloid, the NOW, was forced to close, ending its 168 year history. During my days (1970) at the Australian National University Graduate, I had for many years looked upon Mr. Murdock with a sense of aspiration, so when this recent news broke out, I could not help but wonder if he had to go to that extent. He is a native of Australia, and although he was young, had bought the London Times, which was the beginning of his future of becoming a multi-national media baron. Later, he progressed into the U.S., recently acquiring the Wall Street Journal. With dominating the media world just within his reach, this scandal occurred. An extremely powerful and influential man, he was feared and humored by Former Prime Ministers. This time, however, Prime Minister Cameron ordered the Metropolitan Police to conduct an investigation. This occurred when Mr. Murdock, being of advanced age, had started to restructure the numerous subsidiaries he owned prior to transferring these to his son and successor, James. However, the die-hard Mr. Murdoch announced his plans to become CEO of News International. When I was young, I had admired Mr. Murdoch, now I will watch to see when he meets with Nemesis.

Pipeline：人材パイプライン）"について触れたが、このタイミングでオリンパス事件が起きた。素晴らしい内視鏡製品という"プロダクト・パイプライン（Product Pipeline）"を持ちながら、"エグゼクティブ・パイプライン"の貧しさから起きた事件である。会社のガバナンスは人であるということを如実に物語っている。真面目な投資家、すぐれた技術者や営業の人達の心境を思うと、内視鏡製造の継続と再起を願ってやまない。

遙かにウォーターゲートビルディング　　　© Stephen Finn - Fotolia.com

Within the third narrative, I touched upon the "Executive Pipeline". This, in relation to the Commandment of "You shall not steal", can be seen in the Olympus incident. In this incident, Company executives set up a massive accounting fraud to cover up $1.7 billion in losses. Although Olympus possessed a fantastic "Product Pipeline", as seen in their endoscopic instruments, it was entirely due to their inadequate, or poor, "Executive Pipeline" that caused this corporate fiasco. This incident clearly reflects that corporate governance is with its people. When I think about the great technical people they have, including their dedicated sales force, I cannot help but wish that Olympus continues its endoscope manufacturing and makes a comeback.

第15話
ウソをついてはいけない

　モーゼ第9の戒めは、"You should not bear false witness.（偽証してはならない）"である。裁判の内外を問わず偽証してはならない、すなわち"ウソをついてはいけない"ということである。ただし、ユダヤの賢者は、例外を認めている。それは、いわゆる"罪のないウソ（white lie）"で、人の感情に配慮してのウソである。例えば、自分の妻が、さほど美人でないと思っていても、「お前は美人だなぁー」と言ってみたり、終末の近い患者を病院に見舞って、現実にどう見えても「ひどいですねー」などと言ってはならないということである。

　偽証で思い出すのは、米国のオリバー・ノース大佐（Oliver Laurence North）である。ノース中佐（退役後は大佐）は米国海軍アカデミーを卒業後、22年間海兵隊に勤務し、ベトナム戦争では負傷したが、米国政府テロ対策のコーディネーターとして、レーガン政権入りした。数々の軍功があった人物である。イラン・コントラ事件、すなわちイラクと戦争中のイランに武器を輸出し、そこで得た資金をニカラグア（共産主義政権）の反政府組織であるコントラに移し、反政府活動を支援する仕組みを構築した人物である。1987年、イラン・コントラ事件を調査する上院・下院協議会のテレビ公聴会に召喚され、証言を行った。公聴会において、当人は両院に対し、偽証したことを認め、告訴され有罪となった。ただ、共産主義の拡大を阻止しようとした行為は正しく、彼の保守

The Fifteenth Narrative

Don't Lie

Moses' Ninth Commandment is, "You should not bear false witness". Regardless as to whether it is within or outside of a trial setting, falsification or perjury is not allowed. Simply, do not lie. Jewish sages allow specific exceptions. What we would refer to as 'white lies', which are not based on malice or deception, but are expressed with consideration toward an individual's feelings, may be permissible in some circumstances. For example, let us say, although your wife may not be a conventional beauty, you may say "You are beautiful". If you visit someone who is near death in the hospital, when you actually see him/her, you certainly don't say "God, you look terrible".

The word 'perjury' brings back memories of Lieutenant Colonel Oliver North (U.S.) of the Iran-Contra Affair. Lieutenant Colonel North had graduated from the United States Naval Academy and had served for 22 years in the Marine Corps. After being wounded in Vietnam, he became deputy director for political-military affairs in the Reagan Administration. His record reflects his numerous military achievements. The Iran Contra Affair entailed supplying Iran with weapons while they were at war with Iraq, and using the profits to support anti-government organizations in Nicaragua, the Contras, in their fight against the Nicaraguan (communist) government. Large parts of this scheme were devised by Lieutenant Colonel North. In 1987, a joint commission of the House Select Committee to Investigate Covert Arms Transactions with Iran and the Senate Select Committee on Secret Military Assistance to Iran held televised hearings to which he was called to testify. He admitted that he had lied to Congress, and he was later tried for this and oth-

的な政治的大義も評価されている。

　この保守的な政治的大義で思い出すのは、本章第14話で取り上げた盗聴事件(ウォーターゲート事件)のニクソン大統領である。ウォーターゲート事件はソ連とのデタントに前向きであったニクソンに対し、保守的な政治大義を目論む保守派が仕掛けた政治的クーデターであるという見方もある。ウォーターゲート事件の当時、ワシントン・ポスト紙が事件の真相を語る情報をしきりに流したことは、衆知のことであるが、その情報源が元FBI副局長であった事実を、マーク・フェルト元副局長(William Mark Felt)本人が、2005年に暴露している。

　1963年11月22日のケネディ暗殺事件も、裏にある種の政治的大義があったのではないかと疑いたくなる。情報公開のタイミングが待たれる。

　何度も書くが、ユダヤの律はエジプトからカナンの地に至る40年の厳しい旅の中で生まれた法であるが、現実もよく見ている。第9の戒めの例外からは、3千年を経た今にも通ずる"厳しさの中の優しさ"を感じる。ここで触れたいのは、がんの告知の問題である。

　筆者は父、母、姉をがんで亡くしている。1970年代と1980年代の両親の際には、本人たちが気付いていても何も言わず、周囲もがんという言葉には触れないままに終末を迎えた。がんすなわち死を意味する時代であったから、皆が我慢したのである。1980年代後半の姉の場合には、姉は告知を受けて混乱し、精神・神経科にもお世話になったが、ホスピスで終末を迎えた。

　現在、日本においても、がんはチーム医療体制ができている。ホスピ

er offenses. His actions to prevent the expansion of communism have since been perceived as correct. Thus his conservative political and noble cause has received appraisal.

When referring to conservative political causes, in narrative 14 I touched upon a specific wiretapping incident (the Watergate Scandal) and President Nixon. There is a view taken by some that the Watergate Scandal was a political coup against the pro-d?tente Nixon, which had been planned by conservatives who wanted to preserve the conservative political cause. At the time of the Watergate Scandal, as everyone is well aware, the Washington Post was fervently publishing information revealing the truth behind the scandal. However, it was not until 2005 that the identity of 'Deep Throat', the source of information, was revealed as former Associate Director of the FBI, Mark Felt.

The assassination of President Kennedy on November 22, 1963, also makes one suspect that there may have been a politically wrong cause that was seeking to benefit some groups acting in the background. We must all await the time when the information is released to the public.

I write again how the Jewish teachings were the result of their exodus from Egypt to Canaan. Although the laws were developed within the harsh and difficult travel that took over 40 years, they were closely looking at reality as well. Take for instance the Ninth Commandment and its exception of the 'white lie'. Even today after 3,000 years, you can feel the gentleness within the harshness. Here I will like to touch upon the issue of informing cancer patients of their diagnosis.

Personally, my father, mother and sister have all succumbed to cancer. In the 1970s and 1980s, when my parents were diagnosed with cancer, although they may have been aware of this, those surrounding them never mentioned the word 'cancer' and they passed away. It was a time when the word 'cancer' meant death, so everyone endured and avoided any discussion of it. Even in the later-half of the 1980s the word "cancer" still had a very powerful impact. In the case of my sister, who upon receiving the cancer diagnosis, experienced

ス役のメンバーもチームに加わり、医師を中心とするチームとして、患者が安心してがんの治療に挑戦できるようになった。本当に良かったと思っている。

a nervous breakdown, which lead to neuropsychiatric treatment, with her final days at a hospice.

Currently even in Japan, cancer treatment is conducted by a physician-centered team with nurses and pharmacists. An individual representing the hospice role also joins the team to provide the patient with a sense of comfort and reassurance and to reinforce the patient's will toward treatment. I am sincerely happy that this system has been established.

第16話

隣の芝生は青くない──羨望を断ち切れ

　モーゼ第10の戒めは、"You shall not covet your neighbor's house.（隣人の家にあるものをむやみに欲しがってはならない）"である。ユダヤの律によれば、人間の業である羨望を断ち切る方法がある。あなたが誰かを羨み、その人物の持ち物を欲しいと思ったとすると、あなたはその人のあらゆる物と交換しなくてはならない。すなわちその人にならなくてはならない。ある人が持っているお金を欲しい、美しい容貌を欲しいとなると、その人自身にならなくてはならない。そうすると、あなたの両親は、その人の両親にならなくてはならない。そんなことが起こるはずがない。愚かなことである。まあ、こんな風に考えることで、羨望の念を断ち切れというのである。面白い発想である。第9話の"An independent thinker（物真似でなく自身で考える）"に通ずる考え方である。

　この第10の戒めは、"否定的戒め（365戒）"の1つである。そしてモーゼは十戒の最後の戒とした。面白いことに、"肯定的戒め（248戒）"に"You shall love your neighbor as yourself.（あなたの隣人を我が身の如く慈しめ）"がある。これは、キリストの教えとしてキリスト教の基本の1つとされている戒めである（新約聖書）。しかし、これはすでに述べた通り、旧約聖書に入っている。もちろんキリストはユダヤ人であるから、この戒めを知っていたはずであるが、キリスト教徒にはこれがキリストの言葉と思っている人がいる。

The Sixteenth Narrative

The Other Man's Grass May Not Be Greener, Sever Thoughts of Envy

The Tenth Commandment of Moses is "You shall not covet your neighbor's house". According to Jewish teachings, there is a way to sever envy, a sin of us human beings. Let us assume that you are envious of a certain individual, and you want to own his possessions. This means that you would have to exchange every imaginable thing with that individual. In short, you would have to become this individual. If you want the money that an individual possesses, or you want the beautiful appearance of a certain person, then you would have to become that person. Your parents must become the other individual's parents. However, this will never happen. It is utterly foolish to even conceive of this happening. Well, it is a way, through thinking of these aspects, to sever thoughts of envy. It is truly a fascinating way to change a mindset. This method of thought, or perception, may be similar to 'An independent thinker' of Narrative No. 9.

This Tenth Commandment is one of the negative lessons (365 lessons). It is also the last Commandment of Moses' Ten Commandments. It is interesting to note that the Commandment "You shall love your neighbor as yourself" is within the affirmative lessons (248 lessons). This lesson is said to be a lesson from Christ, and is one of the fundamental teachings of the Christian faith (New Testament). However, as I have noted previously, this Commandment existed in the Old Testament. Of course, Christ being Jewish would have been familiar with this Commandment, but there may be Christians who believe that these were originally the words of Christ.

Although I have written that envy is a human sin, it is an emotion that

羨望は人間の業であると書いたが、これに纏わる人間模様には例を事欠かない。ここで、羨望される側が、羨望する側を手玉にとった例を述べたい。海千山千のダライ・ラマ14世（Dalai Lama、1935年〜）の話である。

　最近のダライ・ラマの素早い動き——チベット亡命政府（1959年〜）の政治的リーダーから降りるという発表——は、羨望の対象としてのダライ・ラマに代わる人物を自らのチベット自治区に任命しようとする中国政府を混乱させるものであった。世界を相手に50余年、亡命政府を維持発展させたダライ・ラマの"したたかさ"である。"世俗・政治（Temporal）"と"宗教・精神（Religious）"両方のカリスマであったダライ・ラマは、その片方を捨て禅譲することで、中国政府の野望を砕くのである。

　また羨望の的になろうとして、願っても願ってもなれなかった男の話がある。織田信長（1534〜1582年）を心から敬愛し、羨んだ豊臣秀吉（1537〜1598年）は、信長亡き後、安土城の豪華絢爛な芸術・工芸を維持発展させたが、朝鮮出兵という過ちを犯して没した。海外情勢に耳を傾け、バテレンの布教を認めた信長の夢を、バテレン追放令（1587年）を出した秀吉が理解するのは無理であった。究極の"ほととぎす"は鳴かなかったのである。信長の夢は、西から東を征服したアレキサンダー大王（紀元前356〜紀元前323年）にならって、逆に東から西をうかがうことであったに違いない。朝鮮から入り、中国・東南アジアを経て中東に至るシルクロードの制圧である。

　ひきかえ徳川家康（1542〜1616年）は、先達から学び、正反対の鎖国という手段で250年以上の平穏と繁栄をもたらした。それだけではない。

cannot be avoided within human events or relationships. Here I will like to give an example where an individual who was envied, took advantage of this emotion and use it against the envious person. This individual is the scrupulous Dalai Lama 14th (76 years old).

The recent Dalai Lama, swiftly announcing that he was stepping down as the political leader of the Tibetan Government in Exile (1959 ~), caused turmoil to the envious Chinese government, which had placed their substitute Dalai Lama in autonomous Tibet. This reflects how the Dalai Lama, who had interacted with the world for almost 50 years for the sustention and growth of the Tibetan Government in Exile, had shown how calculating he could be. Being the charismatic secular and religious leader of Tibet, by totally separating himself from the secular autonomous Tibet and executing a peaceful transfer of power, the Dalai Lama broke the ambitions of the Chinese Government.

I would also like to present a tale of a Japanese man who wanted to be envied, wishing and wishing for this, but who did not accomplish the status. This man, who loved and envied Nobunaga Oda (1534 ~ 1582) from the bottom of his heart, was Hideyoshi Toyotomi (1537 ~ 1598). After the death of Nobunaga, Hideyoshi sustained and developed the fabulous arts and crafts of Azuchi Castle. However, after committing a huge mistake of invading Korea, he died. Nobunaga, who had shown a great interest for information from abroad, had allowed the padres to conduct missionary work. On the other hand, Hideyoshi ordered a ban on padres (1587) because he could not perceive what Nobunaga's dream really was. It seems that the cuckoo didn't sing (that is, didn't bring a message of good tidings). Nobunaga's dream was similar to that of Alexander the Great (BC 356 ~ BC 323), who had conquered from the West to the East. The only difference was that Nobunaga conquered from the East to the West. His plan was to go in from Korea, then to proceed to China/Southeast Asia and into the Middle East, ultimately controlling the Silk Road.

Contrary to this would be the efforts of Tokugawa, Eiyasu (1542 ~

徳川家は尊王開国という時の流れ（明治維新）にも巧みに乗り、明治政府では侯爵として残った。"ほととぎす"は鳴いたのである。

ホトトギス

織田信長
豊臣秀吉
には、鳴かなかった

鳴かせたのは
徳川家康
ダライ・ラマ

1616). He learned from his elders and took the totally opposite approach of isolating the Japanese country. This brought peace and prosperity to the nation for over 250 years. However, his legacy did not stop there. The Tokugawa dynasty skillfully survived through the Meiji Restoration that brought in a renewed reverence and power to the Emperor and opened Japan to other nations of the world, while receiving the title of marquis from the Meiji government. The cuckoo sang.

第17話
足るを知る人は心豊かなり

　モーゼ第10の戒めは、"You shall not covet your neighbor's house.（隣人の家にあるものをむやみに欲しがってはいけない）"であるが、この"covet（羨望）"と全く縁がない、是非とも触れておきたい人がいる。中国人でフィナンシャル・タイムズ（Financial Time）の週末版のコラムを書いているデヴィット・タン卿（Sir David Tang）である。

　氏は、広東省南海出身の、香港で財を成した鄧志昂（トウ・シボウ）の曾孫である。起業家・実業家・慈善家にして社交界の名士である。洋の東西を問わず、文化に対する見識は見事と言わざるを得ない。羨望というものをまったく感じさせず、全てに満ち足りた、豊かな心の持ち主である。北京語で彼の名は、鄧永鏘（デン・ヨンギャン）である。と言えば、誰でも思い浮かべるのは有名な鄧小平（デン・シャオピン）であろう。筆者は確認する術を持たないが、デヴィット・タン卿（Sir David Tang）はその姓から、東洋のユダヤ人と言われる客家人（ハッカ人）なのかもしれない。客家人については高木桂蔵氏の『客家』（講談社現代新書、1991年）が詳しい。かつて中原（黄河流域）の漢民族であったが、いく度かの移動によって、現在は揚子江を南下した四川省、広東省、福建省など南中国一帯に広く住むという。

　客家人は、その人脈を見ると、凄さがわかろうというものである。清

The Seventeenth Narrative

Learn To Be Contended

Moses' Tenth Commandment is, "You shall not covet your neighbor's house". The word 'covet', which I have no need to dwell on, brings me to touch upon a certain individual. It is Sir David Tang who writes a column for the weekend Financial Times.

Sir Tang is the great grandson of Tang Chi-gong, who hailed from China's Guangzhou Nan Hai Province, and later built a fortune and became one of the most successful businessmen in Hong Kong. Sir Tang is well known as an extremely successful businessman, philanthropist, and socialite. His understanding of culture is nothing but outstanding, and he possesses the persona of a totally fulfilled individual who is totally devoid of envy. In Mandarin his name is Deng Yongqiang. The Deng name, as anyone would immediately recognize, is also held by another esteemed individual Deng Xiaoping. Although I have no way of confirming my assumption, however, with the surname of 'Deng', it is very possible that Sir David Tang is a member of the Hakka people, who were often referred to as Asian Jews. Mr. Kenzo Takagi, who wrote a book entitled "Hakka", published by Kohdansha in 1991, would be far more informed on the subject. It is said that the Hakka were a subgroup of the Han Chinese, who through the centuries migrated numerous times. Now many are residing south of the Yangzi River across the vast area of south China, in Provinces such as Sichuan, Guangdong and Fujian.

If we take a look at the network of notable Hakka people, it is easy to recognize that it extremely impressive. This network includes the revolutionary Sun Yat-sen who led the Xinhai Revolution overthrowing the Qing Dy-

朝崩壊のきっかけとなった辛亥革命の立役者である孫文（その妻の宋慶齢、妹で蒋介石の妻である宋美齢）をはじめ、葉剣英（ヨウ・ケンエイ、人民解放軍統括）、林彪（リン・ピョウ）、鄧小平（トウ・ショウヘイ）、李鵬（リ・ホウ、周恩来の養子）、さらに海外においてはシンガポール国家創設の李光耀（リー・クァンユー）、その後継者呉作棟（ゴー・チョクトン）、台湾の李登輝（リ・トウキ）、タイの元首相タクシン氏、その妹で現首相のインラック氏などがいる。ユダヤの民は、その律(Torah：戒め)を通じて、2500年余り、国家がなくとも民としての心の統一を成し遂げ、イスラエル建国（1948年）に至ったのである。何を手段に、客家の人達は横の連繋を保つことができたのであろうか。高木桂蔵氏によると、客家語(口語)というものがあり、それは北京語・広東語を話す人々にも理解できないという。この客家語こそが、自分達だけのコミュニケーションの手段として、客家の団結と共生を成し遂げさせているのである。客家の性格は、ユダヤの人々によく似ている。起業家精神・教育熱心・闘争心・慈善家・正直であることなど、まさに"東洋のユダヤ人"と言っても過言ではない。

　話をデヴィット・タン卿(Sir David Tang)に戻そう。氏は、香港のラサール小学校 (La Salle) で教育を受けたという。同校は、遡って1680年にフランスで設立されたローマカトリック系の学校である（体罰を禁じていることで有名）。その後に13歳で、英国で有名な独立系中・高一貫校パース・スクール・ケンブリッジ(The Perse School Cambridge)に送られている。1615年創立の伝統校である。そこからロンドン大学のキングスカレッジで学び、ケンブリッジ大学で法律を修めている。その出自と共に子供の時からの独特の教育方針により、なるべき人になったのであろう。氏の凄いところは、いわゆる欧米民主国家におけるネットワークだけではなく、1991年にはキューバ葉巻ブランドであるコヒーバ (Cohiba) の

nasty, his wife, Soong Chin-ling, her sister, Soong May-ling (wife of Chiang Kai-shek), Ye Jianying, Lin Biao (Chinese Communist general), Deng Xiaoping, and Li Peng (adopted son of Zhou Enlai). Looking outside of China, the network includes Singapore's founding father, Lee Kuan Yew, his successor Goh Chok Tong, Taiwan's Lee Teng-hui, Thailand's former Prime Minister Thaksin Shinawatra, and his sister and current Prime Minister Yinglak Shinawatra, among others. Through teachings of the Torah, the Jewish people, without a homeland, had succeeded in sustaining a common unity as a people for nearly 2,500 years, which ultimately led to founding the nation of Israel (1948). What supported and sustained the network linkage of the Hakka people? According to Mr. Kenzo Takagi, there was a Hakka spoken language that could not be understood by those who spoke Mandarin or Cantonese. This Hakka spoken language was their unique method of communicating, and they succeeded through the principle of solidarity and coexistence. Their attributes are amazing, being very similar to the Jewish people. They mutually possess the entrepreneurial spirit, and place importance on education. They tend to be competitive, philanthropists, and honest, among other traits. Understandably it is easy to see why the Hakka people are at times referred to as the Asia Jews.

Going back to Sir David Tang, he received his education at Hong Kong's La Salle Primary School. The history of this school goes back to 1680 when it was established by the French as a Roman Catholic school, and is famous for restricting corporal punishment. Later, at the age of 13, he was sent to the private Perse School Cambridge of the U.K. Founded in 1615, it is also an educational institution with a long tradition. From there, he went on to King's College, London, then moved to Cambridge where he studied law. Combined with his background and unique educational line, it is only natural that he became what he is today. What is particularly unique about Sir Tang is that in addition to his network to the western democratic nations, in 1991 he became the exclusive distributor of the Cuban cigar brand Cohiba, which led to his being awarded the title of Honorary Consul of Cuba in

代理権を取得し、香港のキューバ名誉領事というタイトルを持っていることでも、おわかりになっていただけると思う。氏は、2003年に英国人ルーシー・ワストネジ（Lucy Wastnage）と再婚しているが、よく"uxorious（奥さん孝行）"という言葉を使う。「それは奥さんベッタリということなのか、それとも奥さんの独立性を認めるということなのか？」と聞かれて、氏曰く「そんなことではないんだ、好きで堪らんのさ！」。また、2008年には大英帝国侯爵（Knight Commander of the Order of the British Empire）をエリザベス女王より授与され、英国貴族に列する、まさにデヴィット・タン卿（Sir David Tang）なのである。

亡妻順子と（2009年）

Hong Kong. In 2003 Sir Tang married to Ms. Lucy Wastnage of the U.K., and often refers to himself as uxorious. Asked whether this refers to his affection toward his wife or that he accepts his wife's independence, his response was, "It's not that, I just love her so much". In 2008, he was awarded the Knight Commander of the Order of the British Empire (KBE) by Queen Elizabeth, aligning himself with British nobility as Sir David Tang.

故次女陽子(1991)

第18話
家族間でお金の貸し借りをしてはならない
―― 十戒余話1

　第17話まで、モーゼの十戒に則って話を進めてきたが、面白いと言ってくれる方もいて、ありがたいかぎりである。エジプト奴隷であったユダヤの民は、モーゼに導かれた出エジプト時代（紀元前1200年頃）から最近まで大変な差別のなかで生きてきた。反ユダヤ主義者や異邦人（ユダヤにとっての外国人）が自らの憎悪や偏見を納得させるために、ユダヤの律法の引用句（Quotes）を利用してきたのである。

　なかでも最もよく誤解のもとになったのが"Eye for eye, tooth for tooth（目には目を、歯には歯を）"である。しかしユダヤの裁判では文字通りの意味で"目には目を〜"を科すことは当然ながらなかった。ではどのように解決していたかというと、加害者はその加害に相応しい金銭を被害者に支払うことで結審していたのである。

　次に"You must not make your brother pay interest.（兄弟に［金を貸したり］利息を払わせてはならない）"がある。古くユダヤの律法では、家族間ではお金を貸すことも利息を取ることも禁じられていた。ここで家族とは、ユダヤの律法を守る人々のことである。ユダヤの民とは、宗教でもなく人種でもないという。モーゼにとっては、カナンの地に向かう40年の道中、100万人単位まで膨れあがったユダヤの民全てが家族であったに違いない。後になってもユダヤ人どうしの間では、金銭のやり

The Eighteenth Narrative

The Ten Commandments and Other Allegories (Part 1) Neither Lends or Barrows Among Family

Up until the Eighteenth narrative, I have written of examples aligned to the Ten Commandments. There are those who have said that the narratives are interesting, to which I am grateful. From the time the Jewish people were slaves in Egypt, and were led by Moses out of Egypt (BC 1200) to recent times, they have lived through various degrees of discrimination, which at times was very severe. Anti-Semitics or gentiles have justified their own hatred and discrimination by exploiting, without fully understanding, quotes from Jewish teachings.

One of the most misinterpreted teachings is "An eye for an eye, tooth for a tooth". For in a Jewish trial, a sentence or penalty of "an eye for eye" was understandably never given or applied. The sentence would be to have the individual at fault adequately compensate the victim monetarily for the damage done.

Another misinterpreted teaching is "You must not make your brother pay interest". From long ago, according to the Torah, the Jewish people were forbidden to conduct monetary transactions, such as loans and interest on loans, within the family. However, what is the family to the Jewish people? It is those who honor, follow and obey the teachings of the Torah. The Jewish people are not based solely upon religion or race. For Moses, it is not hard to image that the entire Jewish people, whose number had expanded to a million and who had followed him for 40 years to Canaan, had become his 'family'. Later, because the Jewish people could not conduct monetary transactions among fellow Jews, they proceeded to develop their financial business through

とりはできず、キリスト教徒や異邦人との間で金融業を営むことになった。例えばフランクフルトのユダヤ人達は、ゲットーに住み、土地を持てず、公職に就けず、職業選択の自由もなかった。効率の良い仕事となると、金融業ということになる。現在でも、ウォールストリートが彼らの活躍の中心の場であるのは、決して偶然ではなく必然だったのである。ヘッジファンドの創始者である慈善家のジョージ・ソロス（George Soros、1930年〜）然りである。

　江戸時代中頃、マイヤー・アムシェル（Meyer Amschel、1744〜1812年）という男児がフランクフルトのユダヤのゲットーで誕生した。彼は少年の頃、ユダヤ教牧師養成学校に通う敬虔なユダヤ教徒であった。後にロスチャイルド家（Rothschild）の祖と呼ばれることになる。彼の事業理念は、"共に勝者(win-win)"であったという。現在でも、ロスチャイルド家の社会福祉への貢献は見事である。彼は10代で独立し、ユダヤ人の間ではできない金融業をキリスト教徒、貴族、軍関係者相手に行い、さらに宮廷にまで手を延ばした。そして大戦の度に蓄財し、世界の大富豪となったが、それには理由があった。

　彼こそが、"グローバリゼーション"の始祖であるのだ。妻との間に、9人の子があり、5人の男児に恵まれた。長男にフランクフルトの本店を任せ、三男をロンドンに、五男をパリに、次男、四男をそれぞれナポリとウィーンに送り、支店を開設させた。時は18世紀である。当時の大国すべてに支店をおき、"世界の情報収集"を行い、次の一手を考えていたのである。200年後の今とまったく変わらない。凄いの一言である。

　そのロスチャイルド・グループに2011年の暮れからこの2012年3月にかけて異変が起きている。この21世紀に向けて、新しい改革が始まっ

conducting transactions with Christians and gentiles. For example, the Jewish residents of Frankfurt were forced to live in ghettos, were not allowed to own property (land), could not apply for public offices, and were not free to choose their occupations. Of the remaining occupations, the financial business took precedence. It is not a coincidence, but an inevitability, that even today Wall Street is a central arena for their operations. An example is Mr. George Soros, philanthropist and originator of the hedge fund.

During the middle of the Edo period in Japan, Meyer Amschel Rothschild (1744 ~ 1812) was a baby boy born in the Jewish ghetto of Frankfurt. Later in his boyhood, as a reflection of his dedication to the Jewish faith, he attended a seminary which taught those who strived to become rabbis. With his business empire to become known as the house of 'Rothschild', his philosophy toward business was 'win-win'. If we look at the contributions made by the 'Rothschild' to social welfare causes, it is nothing short of amazing. Mayer became independent in his teens. With the restriction of not being able to do monetary transactions among his fellow Jews, he started his financial business dealings with Christians, gentiles and military personnel, later to develop into transactions with the Court of Wilhelm of Hesse. It was through major military conflicts, particularly the French Revolution in which he conducted banking services, that he accumulated a vast fortune of a global scale. There is a reason behind this.

He is the founder of the concept of 'globalization'. Mayer and his wife were blessed with nine children, of which five were sons. The eldest son later succeeded his father in overseeing the main house of business in Frankfurt. He sent his third son to London, fifth son to Paris, second son to Napoli, and fourth son to Vienna, establishing branches of the Rothschild business across Europe. The period was the 18th century. At the time, he was establishing branches in major nations, gathering information on a global scale, and thinking of his next move. Even now, 200 years later, nothing has changed, with the Rothschild business empire managing great wealth and spanning the globe. Amazing is all that can be said.

たのである。グループ総帥であるパリのロスチャイルド家出身のデヴィッド・ド・ロスチャイルド（David de Rothschild）がフランス・英国のロスチャイルド金融系を統合するため、自らグループCEOを辞して会長に就任し、グループCEOに"外部出身（non-family）"であるジョン・ローズ卿（Sir John Rose）を任命した。その傘下にフランス・英国組織をおき、フランス出身のオリヴィール・ペコー氏（Olivier Pecoux）、英国出身のニゲル・ヒギンス氏（Nigel Higgins）をそれぞれトップとして任命し、新時代に相応しい体制にするという。ユダヤの知恵の見せ所に、注目だ。

From late last year to this March, unusual events have been occurring at the Rothschild Group. In preparing for the 21 century, new reformations were starting to take place. The head of the Group, David de Rothschild, who is of the Paris based Rothschild family, in a move to combine the French and U.K. Rothschild financial businesses, stepped down as CEO to become Chairman. He appointed Sir John Rose as the Group's non-family CEO. Established under the group were organizations for France and the U.K. To lead these organizations, Frenchman Olivier Pécoux and Englishman Nigel Higgins were respectively appointed. These actions are focused toward building a structure fit for a new age. Attention is to be given to the wisdom of the Jewish people.

第19話

眞の愛と憎しみとは
―― 十戒余話2

　ユダヤの律(旧約聖書)で、作り話・ゆがめられた話として伝わるものに、"God is a Man of War（[ユダヤの]神は、報復を好む）"がある。一方、新約聖書では"神は愛である"という。この違いがまたユダヤの神に対する誤解を増長したのである。ユダヤの考えによると、"感情(emotions)"には序列がない。愛、憎しみ、誇り、寛容などに優劣はなく、みな同じレベルのものであるという。感情とは、時に医薬品のようなもので、その用量により副作用にならぬよう投与されるものである。種々の感情が上手く機能して、初めて人の道が保たれるのであろう。

　ユダヤの律では、愛とは状況により真に必要なものであるが、また愛とはどう考えても間違っていることもあるという。同様に、時により憎しみは悪いことであるが、憎しみを必要とすることもあるという。とにかくユダヤの人にとって、その神とは見えなくても、すべての状況に合わせて判断をする存在であるらしい。

　憎しみが必要であった例を挙げたい。忘れもしない2001年の9.11 (Nine Eleven、2001年9月11日)である。もちろん、それはイスラム教やイスラム教徒への憎しみではない。テロリズムへの憎しみとその実行者への憎しみである。さらに犠牲者への愛と国家としての誇りある決断がある。種々の感情がうまく噛み合い米国自身が納得し、科学技術の進

The Nineteenth Narrative

The Ten Commandments and Other Allegories (Part 2) True Love and Hate

There is what may be referred to as a fable or a warped interpretation in the Jewish teachings (the Old Testaments). It is "God is a Man of War". On the other hand in the New Testaments, there is the teaching "God is Love". This has increased the misunderstanding toward the Jewish God. The Jewish perception toward emotions is that there is no specific ranking. Love, hate, pride, and forgiveness, among many other emotions, are considered equally at the same level. Emotions are similar to medicine, which must be taken in moderation to avoid side effects. It is perhaps with the various emotions functioning well that an individual can sustain a balanced existence.

In the Jewish teachings, love, depending upon the circumstances, is an essential necessity. However, the teachings also note that no matter how you look at it, love may be a mistake. Similarly, hatred is usually seen as a bad emotion to have, but there are times that feelings of hatred are a necessity. In short, for the Jewish people, although they may not be able to see God, its presence is within the decisions made according to any given circumstances.

I would like to give an example of when hatred is a necessity. It is the unforgettable acts that occurred on September 11, 2001, when the World Trade Center and the U.S. Pentagon were attacked by terrorists. Of course this is not hatred toward Islam or those of the Islamic faith. It is hatred toward terrorism and the terrorists who executed the atrocity. Simultaneously we feel compassion toward the victims, and the proud decision made by the nation. Through digesting these various emotions, the United States came to terms with itself. Supported with the progress of scientific technology, on May 2,

歩の裏付けがあって、オサマ・ビン・ラディンは2011年5月2日（米国現地時間5月1日）に、消されたのである。2001年9月11日当日、米国研究製薬工業協会（PhRMA）の国際部門の会議がワシントンで開かれていたが、筆者（当時、PhRMA日本技術代表）は、なぜか出席を直前にキャンセルしていた。また阪神・淡路大地震の1995年1月17日（火）の当日は、アップジョン（Upjohn）からリリー（Lilly）に移りリリー・ジャパン（Lilly Japan、神戸）に初めて挨拶に行く日であった。ところが、前週の木曜日に、当時の支社長ミロン氏より、多忙のため訪問を1週間延ばしてくれと言われ、なぜか神戸に行けなかったのだ。すべてが、偶然ではなく必然で起きていると信じているのだが、その必然は何だったのだろうか。

またユダヤの律の中にある、"You shall not lie with a man as with a woman: It is an abomination（男に女であると嘘をついてはいけない：それは憎悪である）"も取り上げるのは難しい話題であるが、ユダヤの律では男性間の同性愛を禁じている。男女の結びが新しい生命を生むのであり、同性では、新しい生命を生むことはないという科学に基づいている。現在では、世界的に同性愛を認める方向にあると思われる。米国では、中絶と並び同性愛の是非が大統領選に影響する。その支持者を取り込むのか、突き放すのか。こんな話もあった。筆者の30年来の友人で同性愛反対者であるA氏は、米国特許庁長官に内定していた。しかし、クリントン大統領は再選を目指し、選挙日1週間前に同性愛支持団体の票田を獲得するために急遽別人を任命するというハプニングがあった。友人は任官を棒に振った。

またロンドンでは、1990年にイヴァン・マッソウ氏（Ivan Massow）が、ゲイ・コミュニティーを支援する財政支援組織（financial advisory firm）

2011, (U.S. time May 1) the U.S. was able to eliminate Osama Bin Laden. On that fateful day, September 11, 2001, the Pharmaceutical Research and Manufacturers Association (PhRMA) was holding their international committee meeting in Washington D.C. Although I was PhRMA's Japan Technology Representative, for some reason I had canceled attending at the last moment which was fortuitous. In another event, on Tuesday, January 17, 1995, the Kobe earthquake occurred. I had just joined Lilly from Upjohn and was scheduled to visit Lilly Japan headquarters in Kobe for my first meetings that day. A week prior on a Thursday, I received word from the then General Manager, Mr. Millon, that they would be quite busy, so he asked if I could delay my trip to Kobe one week. Thus, I was not there when the great quake shook Kobe. I believe that these are not coincidences, but inevitable occurrences. If so, what caused these inevitable events?

A further Jewish teaching is "You shall not lie with a man as with a woman: It is an abomination". Although this is a rather difficult issue to approach, in the Jewish teachings homosexuality is forbidden. It is through a man and a woman, bound by marriage, that a new life is brought into this world. A couple of the same sex cannot bring a new life into this world, and this is based on science. Currently, it can be seen that there is a global move toward allowing same-sex relationships. In the United States, the issue of same-sex relationships lines up equally with abortions as to influencing the elections for the Presidency. Will candidates try to get the votes of same-sex relationship supporters, or shun them? There is this story. A friend of over 30 years, Mr. A was against same-sex relationships. He was being considered for the post of Director of the United States Patent and Trademark Office. However, President Clinton was running for re-election. One week prior to the elections, in a move to capture votes from an organization supporting same-sex relationships, he suddenly decided to appoint another person as Director. My friend had lost his chance.

In London during the 1990s, Ivan Massow established a financial advisory firm for his support toward the gay community. Every month payments to

を立ち上げている。400ポンドを毎月支給して、若手芸術家を育てている。世界が、色々な意味で多様化している証左でもある。

the amount of 400 pounds were made to nurture young artists. This is proof that the world is becoming, in many respects, multifaceted.

第20話

ブレンド化された民
── 十戒余話3

　今まで旧約聖書によるモーゼの十戒に沿って話を進めてきた。ダビデ王、ソロモン王（紀元前10世紀）の栄光の時を過ぎ、紀元前586年、ソロモン王が創建した第一神殿がバビロニア（ペルシャ）に破壊される。その際、首都バビロンの幽因の身となったユダヤの人々は、アレキサンダー大王によるペルシャの征服（紀元前334年）により解放されて、カナンの地に戻ることができた。アレキサンダー大王によるギリシャ化を経て、その死後ローマの支配下になったが、ローマ市民権を得るのは、ローマ皇帝カラカラの治世（212年）になってからのことであった。今回は、幾多の"離散（diaspora）"を繰り返し、現在の"ブレンドされたユダヤ社会（Blended Jewish Community）"に至るまでのユダヤの流れに触れていく。これを読んでくれる方々が、ユダヤ人に限らず、グローバルな人々とビジネスやプライベートで時を過ごす際には、何かの役に立つだろう。

　まず、アシュケナージ（Ashkenazi）と呼ばれるのは、ドイツのライン川沿いに移住発展したユダヤの人々である。十字軍が盛んであった8世紀には全ユダヤ人口の3％に過ぎなかったのに、さらにボヘミヤ（チェコ）、ハンガリー、ポーランド、ベラルーシ、リトアニア、ロシア、ウクライナなどへ11〜19世紀にかけて大移動した。アシュケナージはホロコースト前の1931年には全体の92％を占めるまでになったという。

The Twentieth Narrative

The Ten Commandments and Other Allegories (Part 3) Blended Community

Up until now, I have narrated stories that are related to the Ten Commandments of Moses according to the Old Testament. The Jewish people flourished during the time of King David and King Solomon (BC 10th Century). However, their days of glory ended, and in BC 586, the First Temple was totally destroyed by the Babylonians (Persia), and the Jewish people were made captives in the capital city of Babylon. When Alexander the Great conquered Persia (BC 334), the Jews were set free, making it possible for their return to Canaan. Alexander the Great introduced Hellenism and Jewish culture was influenced by Hellenistic philosophy. After his death, the Jews came under the rule of the Roman Empire, but they did not become Roman citizens until the rule of Roman Emperor Caracalla (AD212). I wish to touch upon the path taken by the Jewish people from the days of repeated diaspora to evolving into the present day, blended Jewish community. For those of you who are reading this narrative, I hope that it may be of some assistance when you are interacting with not only Jewish people, but people of all ethnic and religious backgrounds either in business or private.

Let me start with the Ashkenazi, Jewish people who had migrated to settle in the area surrounding the Rhine in Germany. After the Crusades, in the 8th century, the Ashkenazi was only 3% of the Jewish population from the 11th to the 19th century, there were large migrations to countries such as Bohemia (Czechoslovakia), Hungary, Poland, Belarus, Lithuania, Russia, and Ukraine. Before the holocaust in 1931, the Ashkenazi population was 92% of the overall Jewish population.

アシュケナージの人々は、イディッシュ（Yiddish）という言葉を使う。これは高地ドイツ地域より発展したドイツ語系の言語であるが、初期の頃はヘブライ語で読み書きされ、異邦人には理解できないコミュニケーション手段である（参照：第1章第17話）。これが律法の実行と共に、異国にあっても団結（Solidarity）を育むのである。筆者は米国の製薬産業界・アカデミアで活躍するアシュケナージの先輩や友人に今でも大変なお世話になっている。

　一方で、イベリア半島（スペイン、ポルトガル）に離散した人々は、セファルディ（Sephardi）と呼ばれる。アシュケナージ同様、独自の言葉であるユダヤ–スペイン語（Judeo-Spanish）を使う。スペイン・ポルトガル古語から発展したラテン系の言葉である。やはり異邦人にはわからない独自のコミュニケーション手段を有しているのである。スペインでは、ユダヤを受け入れたイスラム文化圏（オスマン）でセファルディが芸術・文化の花を開かせた。その流れは近代まで続き、スペインがピカソやダリを輩出したのはご存じの通りである。

　しかし、1096年に始まるキリスト教国の十字軍遠征により、セファルディ、アシュケナージは共に大変な迫害を受けている。特にスペインでは有名なアルハンブラ条令（1492年）により、ユダヤ人はまた離散を余儀なくされた。イスタンブール、モロッコ、アルジェリアへの移住者、ヨーロッパ（イギリス、オランダ、フランスなど）への移住者、キリスト教に改宗（マラーノと呼ばれ蔑まれた）しスペインに残った人々、隠れユダヤ（Crypto-Jews）として同じくスペインに残った人々などに分かれた。

　セファルディ出身で現役を引退した製薬産業元CEOに、筆者は今でもネットワークで大変お世話になっている。

The Ashkenazi people spoke in diversified Yiddish, which was a form of High German. However, they wrote and read in Hebrew, a communication method which the gentiles could not understand. (Refer to Narrative No. 17/ Hakka language) In this manner, they were able to observe the teachings of the Jewish faith, and although in a foreign land, were able to nurture solidarity. I, myself, have Ashkenazi friends and experienced seniors, who are active in the U.S. pharmaceutical industry and academia such as Dr.Norm Marshall et al. They have shown, even today, a great deal of kindness and consideration toward me, for which I am extremely grateful.

Another example is the Sephardi who migrated to the Iberian Peninsula (Spain, Portugal). Similar to the Ashkenazi, they had their own unique spoken language, Judeo-Spanish. It is a form of Latin, which had developed from old style Spanish and Portuguese. Again, they were communicating in a method which could not be understood by the gentiles of the area. It was through the acceptance of the Jewish people that Spain, at the time an Islamic (Osman) nation, experienced the blossoming of crafts and culture. This development was seen recently through the appearances of Spain's Picasso and Dali, which we all know.

However, in 1096 when the Catholic Church broadened the expeditionary wars conducted by the Crusaders, both the Ashkenazi and Sephardi experienced severe persecution. In particular, there is the infamous Alhambra Decree (1492) which ordered the expulsion of Jews from the Kingdom of Castile and Aragon. There were those who migrated to Istanbul, Morocco, and Algeria, and those who migrated to Europe (England, Holland, and France, among others). There were two groups who remained in Spain: those who had converted to Christianity (referred to as Marranos a derogatory term) and those became Crypto Jews.

There is a retired CEO of Sephardi decent in the pharmaceutical industry, and even today, I am extremely fortunate to benefit from this gentleman's network.

Going into the 20th century, there were the Pogroms, which were the

さらに20世紀に入ると、ポグロム（Pogrom：計画的組織的虐殺）がロシア帝国を中心に起こった。もちろん最も悲惨なホロコーストの始まりとなったのは、ナチスによるベルリンの水晶の夜（Crystal Night、1938年11月9日夜～10日夜明け）であるが、ポグロムによって多くのユダヤ人がロシアから米国に離散した。筆者が米国アップジョン社時代に大変可愛がってくれたCEOの故テット・クーパー（late Dr. Ted Cooper）の父親は、この時、ロシアから移民としてニューヨークに来た1人であった（参照：第1章第1話）。

ユダヤの民をバビロンの幽囚から解放した（紀元前334年）アレキサンダー大王
© Lefteris Papaulakis - Fotolia.com

strategically organized violent acts of crimes against the Jewish people by the Russian empire. Of course the most tragic event, later leading to the holocaust, was the Crystal Night. During this infamous event, coordinated by the Nazis in Berlin, attacks were made on Jews from the night of November 9 to the dawn of November 10, 1938, which caused many Jewish people to migrate from Russia to the United States. When I was at Upjohn of the U.S., I interacted with the CEO, the late Dr. Ted Cooper, who took great care of me. His father was one of those who had emigrated from Russia to New York at this time. (Refer to Narrative No. 1).

第21話

ゲノム解析
―― 十戒余話4

　今回は国際ゲノムプロジェクトによるゲノム解析について触れたい。前回述べたユダヤ社会、特にイスラエル国家の外で暮らす人々が、他のヨーロッパ人とゲノム解析上どのような関係にあるかを見たいからである。

　ご存じのごとく、2000年6月26日午前（米時間帯）、クリントン大統領がホワイトハウスから記者会見（TV中継）を行い、米国立ゲノム研究所長のコリンズ博士（Dr. Francis Collins、現NIH所長）と、セレラ社（Celera）代表のベンター博士（Dr. Craig Venter）を紹介し、国際ゲノムプロジェクト（米国を中心にイギリス、日本、ドイツ、フランス、中国が参画）のゲノム解析結果を公表した。

　このように、米国が中心になるのは米国の科学力・資金力、そして特にヨーロッパからの移民国家という背景があるためである。米国にはヨーロッパ各国、アフリカ、アジア、ヒスパニックの移民が住んでおり、これほどゲノム解析に恵まれた国はない。

　ここで2つの論文に触れたい。まず、M.F.セルディン等（M. F. Seldin et al. PLoS Genet. 2006 Sep 15；2 (a) e143）の報告において、5000以上の一塩基多型（SNP：Single Nucleotide Polymorphism）を用いたゲノム解析

The Twentieth-First Narrative

The Ten Commandments and Other Allegories (Part 4) Genetic Analysis

Within this narrative I would like to touch upon the genome mapping undertaken through the international genome project. In the previous narrative I had written of the Jewish society, especially of those who lived outside of the Israeli nation. Now I would like to discuss how they relate to other Europeans in terms of genome mapping.

As many of you may recall, on June 26, 2000 (U.S. time) President Clinton held a televised press conference at the White House, in which he introduced National Human Genome Research Institute Director, Dr. Francis Collins (currently U.S. NIH Director), and Dr. Craig Venter, President of Celera. These individuals described the human genome project (formally begun in 1990 and centralized in the U.S., with the U.K., Japan, Germany, France and China participating) and announced the results of the genome mapping.

This event, presenting studies centralized in the U.S., discussed how the United States, through its scientific and financial strength, was able to determine that it is a nation largely comprised of European immigrants. The United States population is formed from those who emigrated from various European countries, as well as those from African, Asian and Hispanic countries, providing an ideal environment for genome mapping.

Here I would like to discuss two research papers. The first is by M.F. Seldin, et al. (PLoS Genet. 2006 Sep 15 ; 2 (9) e 143), in which it was reported that from the genome mapping of over 5,000 SNP (Single Nucleotide Polymorphism) two major groups were found within the continental Europe-

では、北・中央・東ヨーロッパ人（英国、スカンジナビアを含む）は90%強で北ヨーロッパ系に、南ヨーロッパ人（地中海、イベリア半島など）は85%強で南ヨーロッパ系に分類できるという。そしてユダヤ人（アシュケナージ、セファルディ）は85%強で南ヨーロッパ系に属するという。歴史的にユダヤの民は地中海が起源であることはわかっているが、ゲノム解析でも裏付けされたということか。2500年余の離散を経ても遺伝子型が変わらなかったのはなぜか。ユダヤの人々が、独特なコミュニケーション手段としてイデッシュやユダヤ－スペイン語を使うことにより、独自に律法を守ってきた事と、異邦人による差別という生活環境が上記の結果を説明しているのではないか。

もう1つの面白い文献、A.L.プライス等（A.L. Price et al. Nat Genet. 2006 Aug; 38（8）: 904-9）によれば、ヨーロッパの人口層別解析を行うと、まず北西グループ（前文献の北ヨーロッパ系）と南東グループ（同じく南ヨーロッパ系）に分類できるという。さらなる解析を行うと南東系が2つに分かれるという。これが何を意味するかは報告にないが、筆者には興味ある解析結果である。

さて、アメリカユダヤ歴史学会によると、米国の最初のユダヤ移民は、1654年、ブラジルからニューアムステルダムに来たユダヤ人23人（セファルディとアシュケナージの混成）であった。これにはオランダのアムステルダムのセファルディを中心にしたユダヤ社会のアドバイスがあったという。しかし、1664年にはイギリス人にオランダ人は追い出され、ニューヨークと市名が変わった。ユダヤ人はニューヨークでも苦労しながら、イギリスからの独立戦争（1775年～）、そして南北戦争（1861年～）に参加して今日に至っている。

an population. One group comprised those people of northern, central and eastern parts of Europe (including England and Scandinavia) in which over 90% are of northern European descent. The other group comprised those from southern Europe (Mediterranean, Iberian Peninsula, among others) in which over 85% were from southern Europe descent. With regard to the Jewish people (Ashkenazi and Sephardi), over 85% were found to be of southern European descent. Historically it was believed that the ancestry of the Jewish people was from the Mediterranean. Now there exists genome mapping which supports this. Why is it that after experiencing numerous Diasporas for over 2,500 years, their genotype has not undergone any substantial changes? It may be thought to be the result of the Jewish people communicating with their individual languages, such as Yiddish and Judeo-Spanish. This enabled them to sustain their culture, faith and teachings even while living in gentile-dominated environments, which were often discriminatory.

Another interesting paper is by A.L. Price, et al. (Nat Genet. 2006 Aug;38 (8) : 904-9), which noted that if a population-stratified sampling were to be conducted of Europe, classifications could be made as a north-eastern group (the previous paper's northern European descent), and a south-eastern group (similarly, southern European descent). If further mapping were to be pursued, the south-eastern group could be classified into two separate groups. Although the paper does not report what this implies, for me the findings are quite intriguing.

According to the American Jewish Historical Society, the first Jewish immigrants to Manhattan Island were 23 Jews from Brazil. They were fleeing from Portuguese reconquest of Dutch possessions in Brazil, and in 1654 settled in New Amsterdam (mixture of Ashkenazi and Sephardi). It is said that it was through the advice of Sephardi Jews, who were at the center of the Jewish society in Amsterdam Holland, that the emigrations took place. However, in 1664 the Dutch were forced out by the English and changed the name of the city to New York. The Jewish community, as well as the rest of the population, endured hardships in New York, including fighting for independence

最後に、この十戒シリーズを2011年1月に始め、10回でおさまらず21話まで来てしまった。次章では新たに『国際人になるためのInsight Track』を始める予定である。読んでくださる方々のお役に立たなくてはと緊張している。

NYの風景　　　　　　　　　　　　　　　© Bastos - Fotolia.com

from England (1775 ~) and participating in the Civil War (1861 ~), which brings us to today.

Lastly, I started this Ten Commandment series in January 2011. Unable to contain it within ten segments, I have completed twenty-one narratives. Through the kind consideration of the editor, I am scheduled to start a new series "Insight Track ? To Become an International Minded Person". I will endeavor, in the hopes that what I write will be of some assistance to those who read the narratives.

第 2 章

国際人になるための Insight Track

Chapter 2.

Insight Track– To Become an Internationally-Minded Person

第1話

目で話す人、耳で話す人、口で話す人
——相手のタイプを見極めよ

　今から25年ほど前（1987年）、米国アップジョン社（Upjohn）のミシガン州カラマズーにあるアップジョン研究所（Upjohn Research Laboratories）の社長（President）であり、アップジョンの副会長（Vice Chairman）であったJ.Mitchel氏にある話をしたが、なかなか返事をくれない。同僚のC.Bibart氏に相談した。「彼は、いくら口で話しても返事はないヨ。メモにして渡すんだ」とアドバイスされた。早速、Eメールで提案してみるとすぐに返事があった。この時、J.M氏は"目で話をする"のだなと気付いた。以後、彼と話す時は必ずワン・ページ・メモを渡して話をした。氏はよくマイクロマネージメントだと批判もされたが、いつ寝ているのかと思う程に熱心な研究者で仕事師でもあった。1990年代の中頃には、当時まだ珍しかった"マネージメント・バイアウト（Management buyout）"を仕掛けるような信頼関係になっていた。夜中に電話があって「トシ・コバヤシ」と答えると、「名前は言ってはいけない。誰かを確かめてから」等々。良い経験をさせてもらった。

　そこで、人には"口で話す人"、"耳で話す人"、"目で話す人"がいるということに気付いた。自分の意志・意見を聞いてもらいたい人が、どのタイプの人かを判断することが大切ということである。自分でわからなかったら友達に聞くのも良い。それにより時間・エネルギーの節約（省エネ）となり、効率が上がる（high productivity）こととなるのである。

Number One

A Person Who Communicates with Their Eyes, a Person Who Communicates with Their Ears, and a Person Who Communicates with Their Mouth

I would like to start by reflecting upon an individual who I had encountered around 25 years ago, in 1987. The individual is Dr. J.Mitchel, who was at the time both President of Upjohn Research Laboratories (URL), located in Kalamazoo, Michigan, and Vice Chairman of The Upjohn Company. Although I would speak to him, it was difficult to get a response. I decided to ask for advice from a colleague Dr. C.Bibart who advised; "He will not respond to anything you say verbally. You will have to place it in written form." I immediately submitted my proposal in an e-mail, to which I received an equally quick response. This is when I realized that Dr. J.M. communicates with his eyes. From that time on, whenever there was a necessity to communicate with Dr. J.M., I would submit a one-page memo. Although he was frequently criticized for being a micro-manager, I would at times wonder when he had time to sleep; he was such a dedicated professional researcher. In the mid-1990s when it was still rather rare, we conducted a MBO (management buyout) together based on a strong trusting relationship. It was an extremely good experience for me.

This brings me to say that I have come to realize that there are people who communicate with their mouths, those who communicate with their ears, and those who communicate with their eyes. In short, if there is an individual to whom you want to convey your thoughts or opinions, it is important to decide what type of communicator the individual is. If you can not come to a decision, it may be helpful to ask mutual friends or acquaintances. An understanding of the method of how an individual communicates will

外資に移る前、私が仕えた日本人社長（三菱系）のS.F氏は、メモを絶対にとらない人であった。ジッと聞いていて、頭にノートがあるのかなと思う程であった。あとでタイミングをみて、あの件はどうなったと鋭く迫ってくるような人である。ニューロンのネットワークが桁外れの"耳で話す人"の典型であった。96歳になったS.F氏と2013年の5月に昼食をご一緒した。耳が少し不自由になったが、ロビーで待つのか、レストランで待つのかなどの指示が飛び、昔と変わらない几帳面さに驚いている。

　"口（ボディー）で話す人"の典型は、アップジョン時代の同僚で、後にファルマシア・アップジョンのチーフ・サイエンティフィック・オフィサー（CSO：chief scientific officer）になったR.Gorman氏である。とにかくよく喋り、手を振り体を動かして熱弁をふるっては、氏の研究方針、マイルストーンなどを説いた。戦略上で会社への不満がある際は、動きを止めて明らかに不快な顔をしながら「そうだろう」と同調を求めたのが懐かしい。彼にはよく助けてもらった。アップジョンの筑波研究所にはよく飛んできて、ビジネス部門との綱引きに手を貸してくれた。"口で話す人"は、感情的になりやすいが、明るい人が多く人情家でもある。「ボブ、君の血液型はO型だナ」と言ったら、ビックリしていた顔も懐かしい。

（注）　話を前述のJ.M氏に戻す。氏は人の話を"目で聞く"が、自らが話す言葉にじっと耳を傾けさせて聞き取らせた後、それをメモにして全体に周知させる役をこなす"耳で話す人"が必要であった。よくしたもので、氏の周りには、7人のVPの他にも、その役割を担うスタッフが常時張り付いていた。Ms. I.F、T.G氏、そして教育学博士のS.E氏など、皆良い人達であった。要は組織として考えるならば、トップとなった人の話すスタイルを把握し、それを補うタイプの人で脇を固めるということである。
　また個人対個人の場合、相手の話すスタイルがわかれば、結果としてコミュニケーショ

save time and energy, resulting in high productivity.

An example of an individual who communicated with his ears is Mr. S.F., the Japanese president I worked for before I moved to a foreign-capital company. Mr. S.F. never took notes. He would simply listen intently, making me wonder if there was a notebook inside his head. Later when the timing was right, he would sharply inquire about the status of a specific subject or matter. It was a perfect example of how an unbelievable network of neurons went into communicating through the ears. I had the opportunity to lunch with the 96-year-old Mr. S.F. in May in 2013. Although his hearing was not what it used to be, he inquired, "Are we going to meet in the lobby, or are we going to meet at the restaurant?" surprising me that his usual attention to details had not changed at all.

A perfect example of a person who communicates with his mouth and body is a colleague with whom I worked during my Upjohn days, and who later became Pharmacia & Upjohn's CSO, Mr. R.Gorman. He was a talker, stressing and making points in his conversation through moving his hands and body. The method in which he reported about his research was to give explanations on milestones, etc. If he felt dissatisfied with the company's

Each characteristic

ンの省エネになる。相手が多忙の場合、わかりやすい1頁のメモを作りポケットに忍ばせておいて、必要と感じたら相手に見せながら話をするのも良い方法である。人に会う時、準備にエネルギーを惜しんではならない。

(注)血液型で性格判断をしているのは、日本くらいである。

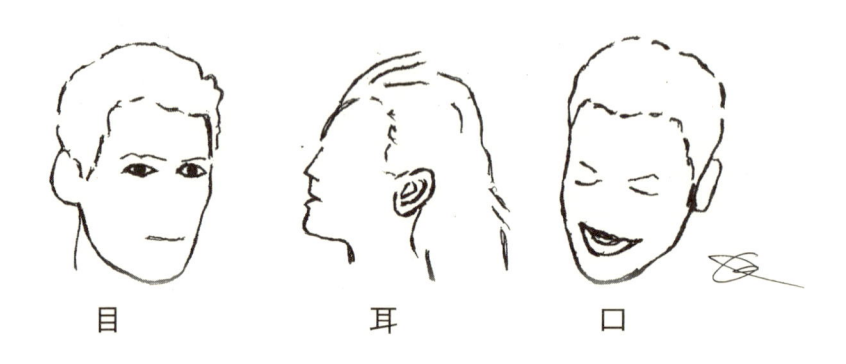

　　　　目　　　　　　　　　耳　　　　　　　　　口

J.Mitchel,President（前列左端／肘掛け）、R.Gorman（後列左から6番目）、C.Bibart（後列右から4番目）ほか Vice P の友人と筆者（前列左から2番目）（1992年）

strategy, his movements would totally stop. Then he would make an expression of distaste and inquire "Don't you think so?" which was accompanied by a look to encourage total agreement. It brings back good memories. He frequently helped me out by flying over to the Upjohn Tsukuba Research Center on numerous occasions to lend me a hand in the tug-of-war with the business division. Individuals who communicate with their mouths easily become emotional, but on a majority they are happy, outgoing, sympathetic people.

I would like to further discuss Dr. J.M. who is referred to in the previous portion of this paper. Although he would listen to people through his eyes, he needed someone who would intently listen to the words that were spoken, and then write it down in a memorandum so that the entirety could be widely distributed. Well, things have a way of working out. He was surrounded by not only 7 VPs, but also a staff that were constantly with him, whose responsibility was to do just that. The staff comprised Ms. I.H., Mr. T.G., and Dr. S.E. (a Doctor of Education); they were all good friends of mine. In short, if you think in terms of an organization, understand the specific style of communication of its leader, and wish to have efficient interactions, it is necessary to put in place the type of people who can fill in the gap and provide appropriate support from the sidelines.

When it comes to person-to-person interactions, understanding the specific style in which an individual communicates results in saving energy. If the individual you wish to communicate with is an extremely busy person, it is helpful to make a very simple one-category note and keep it in your pocket. Then you will have your issues clear in your mind and can present them succinctly. If you think it's necessary, you can also show the memo to the individual as you are speaking to him/her. When preparing to meet with someone, don't save energy. Do what is needed to be thoroughly ready.

第2話

天とは何か

　オーストラリア国立大学から戻った1970年、恩師の山田俊一先生より「小林君、他人(ヒト)の2倍働きなさい。天は見捨てないよ」と言われた。医薬事業を再開する財閥系石油化学会社に行くことになり、先生と同行した車がちょうど湯島天神にさしかかったあたりのことであった。

　1970年から現在に至るまで5回の転職を経験することになった。いずれも落下傘よろしく単独で就任した。幸い撃ち落とされることもなく、後に友人となる多くの部下を持つ責任ある立場で新規事業を立ち上げるという恵まれた環境でもあった。1985年には医薬事業が同一財閥系列の化学会社に合併されることとなり、そのあまりの落差に、半年の後、男の意地"一寸の虫にも、五分の魂"で転職を決意して、最初の敗者復活戦に挑むことになった。

　幸いにして海外関係の仕事をしていたので、海外の友人、有名人材会社から引く手はあまたあり、米国中西部のトップ10会社に移ることになった。ここでの仕事は、筑波学園都市に新しく建設する研究所（200億円）の研究者を採用することとその充実をはかることを、東洋と西洋の文化の融合を心掛けながら達成することであった。

　西洋哲学の代表であるギリシャのソクラテスの言葉"汝、知らざるを

Number Two

What is Heaven?

In 1970, when I returned to Japan from my tenure at Australian National University, my mentor, Dr. Shuichi Yamada, told me "Kobayashi, work twice as hard as anyone else. Heaven will not forsake you." He said this when I had made a decision to join a zaibatsu-related petro-chemical company which was restarting their pharmaceutical business. We were traveling together in a car that was just nearing Yushima Tenjin.

From 1970 to the present, I have experienced 5 job changes. However, all were what I would call 'parachute jumps', in which I alone submitted my letter of resignation. It was then up to the organization to replace me and continue on its path to success. Luckily, I was never shot down, and I was always able to land on my feet. I was given the responsibility to establish and launch a new business, and was surrounded with numerous workers who have become lasting friends. I can say that I was blessed with good working environments. First, in 1985 the pharmaceutical business of the zaibatsu-related petro-chemical firm was taken over by its parent chemical company. Six months later, I found the differences to be so great that I did not think I could continue to work there. Let's face it, a man has his pride. As the Japanese proverb goes 'even the smallest insect has a soul.' I decided to resign, and it was my first challenge toward establishing a re-match in my career.

I was fortunate since I had been working with businesses overseas, and with friends abroad. I had offers through a renowned human resource placement firm and was soon employed by one of the top ten companies located in the mid-west of the United States. My job there was to employ and fulfill re-

知れ"の理詰めに対し、東洋の美徳としては"素心（唐代の書家・顔真卿の言葉で、ものに動じない平常心、正直な心）"（参照：第1話第8章）を選ぶこととした。以降、"素心"こそ、私の座右の銘となった。

当時日米EU医薬品規制会議（1990年）もなく、日米規制の違いの中で、研究プログラムの日米調整、人材・人財の生かし方についてなど難題が毎日続いた。しかし不思議なことに、必ずスーッとうまく解決していくことに気付いた。よく状況分析をしてみると、助けてくれたのは米国の上司であったり、日本人のスタッフであったりと、周りの身近な人達であった。

ここで、山田先生がおっしゃった"天は見捨てない"の"天"というのは"身近な人達"であるということに気付き、まさに目からウロコであった。①競争の激しい成長分野を選択する、②何事も正直に誠心誠意（透明性）を尽くす、③知人・友人と長くお付き合いする（100人の知人は100人の異なった先生、1000人は1000人の先生である）、の3つを心得ていれば敗者復活戦では必ず勝てると思うようになれた。日本の友はもちろんのことだが、この生き方は欧米でも通用し、多くの海外の友人が助けてくれるようになった。一方では、苦々しく思う人も増えたであろうが、そこはM&Aビジネスルール同様、51％のサポートがあれば十分である。

1994年には、アップジョン社CEOテッド・クーパー博士（Ted Cooper）の急逝とともに、我々7人のVPが推したVice Chairmanは敗れ、1人を除き6人が転職を余儀なくされた。しかし、天（友人）は見捨てなかった。私は早速、同じ中西部のトップ10会社に移ることになった。ここでは前会社のCEOのNIH時代にスタッフであったG.W氏がCSO

searchers necessary for a new research facility (20 billion yen) which was to be built at the Tsukuba Science City. One of our missions was to consciously endeavor to combine eastern and western cultures.

Greece's Socrates, as an example of western civilization philosophy, said "The only true wisdom is in knowing that you know nothing." In comparison, reflecting the oriental civilization's philosophy are the words 'So-Shin,' coined by the noted Tang dynasty calligrapher Yan Zhenging. 'So-Shin' encompasses the principle of retaining one's self at all times, and choosing a path of honesty. I have selected 'So-Shin' as my pillar of principle.

In those days, which was before the International Conference on Harmonisation of Technical Requirements for Registration of Pharmaceuticals for Human Use (ICH) when there was a great difference between U.S. and Japanese regulations, it was a daily challenge to coordinate a research program between U.S. and Japanese entities, while ensuring that the human resources/human capital was fully utilized. However, it was rather strange to realize that things were progressing rather smoothly. Wanting to learn why, I began to analyze the situation. I came to realize that in some cases it was because of the support of my superior in the United States, and in other cases, it was because of the staff in Japan. In short, it was through the support of those who were close to me at the time.

It was through this experience that the words of Dr. Yamada, from 1970, came back to me: "Heaven will not forsake you." I realized that 'Heaven' is in fact the 'People Close to Me.' It really opened my eyes. I believe in (1)choosing an extremely competitive growing sector; (2)conducting all matters honestly, and with integrity, sincerity, and transparency; and (3)having long-term relations with acquaintances and friends. If you have 100 acquaintances, it means that you have 100 different teachers. Likewise, if you have 1,000 acquaintances, you have 1,000 teachers. With these principles, I believed that I could definitely win the return match into my career. My Japanese friends, certainly, and since this principle of existence is also known in Europe and the U.S., many of my friends abroad offered me support and help. I cannot deny

の地位にあり、温かく迎えてくれた。役員面接で知り合った同じく有機化学者であったJ.レックライター氏は、現在この会社のCEOを務めており、今でも親交が続いている。

　1人でできることは高が知れており、助けてくれるのは友人・知人・家族であったり、見知らぬ人であったりするものである。前述した①〜③を是非おすすめしたい。

孫5人のおやつの時間(2007年)

that there may have been an increase in the number of those who harbored ill thoughts. However then I considered the terms of the business rule during a corporate merger or acquisition: if you have 51% supporting the deal, that's enough.

In 1994 with the sudden death of CEO Dr. T.C., the Vice Chairman that we seven VPs supported lost during the subsequent corporate struggles. This resulted in six of us facing a job change. Again, however, 'Heaven' and 'Friends' did not forsake me. Immediately, I was able to secure a position with another of the top 10 Mid-western firms. It was here that I was warmly welcomed by Dr. G.W., who was CSO at that time, and who happened to be a member of the NIH staff when my previous company's CEO was at NIH. I met Dr. J.L., who was also an organic chemist, at the Board members' interview. He is currently the CEO of this firm, and we still keep in touch.

In short, there is a limit to what one person can achieve. There are friends, acquaintances, family, and at times those who you have not even met, who are there to give support. I strongly suggest the aforementioned points (1) ∼ (3) as a guiding philosophy.

第3話

誠心誠意——モスクワの友人A.グルシコフ氏

　1973年、国際純正・応用化学連合（IUPAC：International Union of Pure and Applied Chemistry、オックスフォード大学）に、大学院の恩師であるA.アルバート教授（オーストラリア国立大学）からの引きがあり、1973年、30代であったが日本学術会議より任命されて、日本代表として医薬化学（Medicinal Chemistry Section）の委員になった。そこにソ連の代表として参加したのがモスクワ医薬・生化学研究所の部門長であったアレキサンダー・グルシコフ氏（Alexander Glushkof）であった。ロンドンでの会議（1978年）では隣り合わせの席になった。戦後、ケンブリッジ大学に留学していた氏と話をしていて、当時の委員長のジョン・カバラ氏（John Cavalla、英代表）に私語を注意されたのをきっかけに親しい友人となった。当時は冷戦の最中（ソ連はブレジネフ政権）であったが、新薬の探索もかねて、グルシコフ氏をモスクワに訪ねることを思いつき、連絡すると、いつでもどうぞとのこと。1981年12月、真冬のモスクワを訪問した。当時はビザがおりると、ホテルを選択する自由はなく、指定のホテルに泊ることになる。空港に到着すると白髪の紳士が現れ、日本語で「コバヤシさんようこそ。（来年の）カレンダーのお土産はありますか？」。こちらはキョトンとするばかりであったが、すべてお調べ済みという感じであった。ホテルでは、チェックインのあと、「鍵は3階で……」と言われ、3階で妙齢の鍵オンナが鍵を渡してくれた。

Number Three
Sincerity, A Friend in Moscow, Dr. Alexander Glushkof

In 1973, when I was in my 30's, through the backing of Professor A. Albert of the Australian National University, who was my postgraduate professor at the International Union of Pure and Applied Chemistry (IUPAC, Oxford University), I was appointed as the Japan representative committee member of the Medicinal Chemistry Section by the Science Council of Japan. Dr. Alexander Glushkof, Director of Moscow's Medical/Biochemical Research Institute, represented the Soviet Union in this organization. During a Section conference in London, I had the pleasure of being seated next to Dr. Glushkof. He shared with me that after the war, while he was studying abroad at Cambridge University, he was cautioned by the then Section Chair, Dr. John Cavalla (representative of the U.K.) (sic), for talking during the session. The cautioning became the catalyst for the two to become close friends. Although still during the days of the Cold War (Brezhnev Regime in the Soviet Union), I took the opportunity to visit Mr. Glushkof in Moscow as part of a quest for new drugs. During this period, when a visa was granted, you did not have a choice of hotels; you stayed in an assigned hotel. When I arrived at the Moscow airport, a white-haired gentleman appeared and in Japanese inquired "Are you Kobayashi-san? Do you have next year's calendar as a gift?" It was an unusual question, which took me off-guard. However, I had the feeling that my belongings had already received a thorough check. At the hotel, after checking in, I was told that the keys to the room were on the third floor. Upon my arriving there, a woman of an indefinable age turned out to be the 'Key' woman, who promptly handed over the key to my room.

次の朝にはモスクワ研から車が来て、所長以下の歓迎を受けた。午前中いっぱいの会議では、お互いの研究内容の説明と次のステップについての報告をし、昼食をごちそうになり、楽しく時を過ごした。終了時には某通信社が写真を撮ってくれて、新聞に載せるという。後程送ってもらった写真は白黒でよく撮れており、今も私の書斎を飾っている。

　次の日、モスクワ市内を歩いて見学してまわり、ボリショイサーカスを楽しんでホテルの部屋に戻ると、例の鍵オンナから電話があった。「遊びに来ないか」と言う。あー来たナ！　当時日本では、上級自衛官がこの手に落ちて、スパイにされて新聞を賑わしていた。科学とはまったく関係ないが、冷戦時代の政治は、利用できる奴は生き馬の目を抜く素早さで徹底的に利用するという現実を体験して、後に役立つことになった。

　前年の1980年、IUPACの会議がスイスのダヴォス（Davos）であり、グルシコフ氏と再会した。夕食を約束し、時間と場所を決めるためにホテルに電話して、部屋に取次いでもらうと、別人が出てきて、グルシコフ氏はダヴォスには来ていないと言う。「冗談じゃない！　先ほど会議で会ったばかりだ」と言うと、グルシコフ氏が電話に出た。2人1組で部屋を取り監視されていたのである。レストランで会うことができた。当時流行していた電卓をあげると喜んで、「エアロフロートのパイロットをしている息子にあげても良いか？」と言う。どうぞ、どうぞ。

　1983年、西独の西ベルリン市の会議では、ソ連から2人来ていたような気がしたが、氏とは席が離れていた。会議終了時に私の席に飛んできて、新聞紙の包みを私の鞄に押し込み、「バイ！バイ！」と言って部屋を後にした。ホテルに帰って開けてみると大きなキャビアの瓶詰であった。これこそグローバリゼーションの神髄（国境を越えてお互いの誠心

The following morning a car from the Moscow Research Center arrived and took me to the Center where I received a welcome from the Director. A meeting was held all morning during which we mutually explained our areas of research, as well as our plans for moving forward. Upon completion of the meeting, a wire service photographed the event, saying that it would be placed in the local newspaper. Later I received the black & white photograph, which was rather well taken and still graces my study. Our sessions were completed after being treated to lunch. I enjoyed the time I experienced there.

The next day I took a walk around the city of Moscow, and spent some enjoyable time at the Bolshoi Circus, after which I returned to my hotel room. I there received a call from the 'Key' woman who asked "Would you like to come and have a good time?" "Ah, here it comes," was my first reaction. I recalled that during this time, a member of the Japanese Self Defense Force had fallen into a similar trap and was labeled a spy. This incident was widely covered by the Japanese newspapers. Although it has nothing to do with science, politics during the Cold War were such that if they thought they could exploit or take advantage of someone, it would happen with unbelievable speed and ruthless thoroughness. I experienced this in reality. However, later this experience proved beneficial.

In 1980, the IUPAC conference was held in Davos, Switzerland, where I had the opportunity to be re-united with Dr. Glushkof. The two of us made a promise to meet for dinner. Wishing to further confirm the time and place, I made a phone call to his hotel. When the call was forwarded to his room, a totally different individual responded saying "Dr. Glushkof did not come to Davos." "You must be joking!" was my response. I continued, "I just met him at the Conference." It was then that Dr. Glushkof came on the phone. It turned out that two individuals as a pair stayed in one room so that observations could be made. We were able to meet at a restaurant, at which time I gave him a then popular calculator, which he seemed truly pleased to receive. He asked, "Can I give it to my son who is a pilot for Aeroflot?" I naturally responded, "Please do, please do."

誠意が結ぶ友情）かと感動を禁じ得なかった。グルシコフ氏はまさに、誠心誠意の人であった。最後はソ連科学アカデミーのトップにまで登りつめた。

モスクワにて（1981年）

Two years later, at the West Berlin conference, I thought that there were again two representatives from the Soviet Union. We were seated apart, making it difficult to confirm the presence of Dr. Glushkof. At the end of the conference, however, he came running to my seat and pushed a newspaper-wrapped object in into my briefcase, saying "Bye, bye", and then left the room. Returning to my hotel, I opened the parcel to find a large bottle of caviar. I felt that this was the true essence of globalization, when a sincere and wholehearted friendship is able to overcome boarders. Recognizing this, I could not help but be moved by the thought of how he was a truly sincere individual.

Saint Basil's Cathedral

第4話
「思いついたらすぐやる」は両刃の剣

　1980年代、千葉県松戸市の市役所に「すぐやる課」という組織があった。当時の市長は松本清氏であったが、氏は「マツモトキヨシ」という薬局チェーンを展開したことで有名である。今では、大手スーパーの一翼を担うマツモトキヨシホールディングスにまで成長している。松戸市の「すぐやる課」こそ、カスタマーサービスの真髄である。市民の日常生活における要望をすぐに実行に移して市民の心をつかんだのである。もちろん、市予算で認められた枠の中でのことであろう。多分、アイデアは自ら思いつくだけではなく、市民に思いつかされることもあったと考えられるが。カスタマーの心を読み、先手を打つサービスこそがカスタマーサービスなのであろう。

　「経営上の思いつき」は、信念のない場合、実行に移すことは甚だ危険である。オーナー社長の場合、往々にしてこの種のことが起き、倒産した会社は数え切れない。思いつきで起業したベンチャーが瞬く間もなく消えていくのも同じである。信念のない思いつきは危ないということである。某新聞に200年企業として取り上げられている企業は、歴代のオーナーの信念と使命感の賜物である。

　10数年前の話であるが、私の知人で米国人であるM.M氏は外資系の日本支社に勤務する課長クラスのマーケティングマンであった。思いつ

Number Four

Act Immediately on Inspirations
——Double-Edged Sward

Inspiration in Service: In the 1980s, within the City Hall of Matsudo City, Chiba Prefecture, there was an organization referred to as the 'Immediate Action Department'. The mayor of the city at the time was Mr. Kiyoshi Matsumoto, who is famous as the founder of the drug store chain 'Matsumoto Kiyoshi'. Today, the business has grown into the league of large-scale supermarkets, having become 'Matsumoto Kiyoshi Holdings'. Matsudo City's 'Immediate Action Department' was the quintessence of customer service. The department's quick actions toward requests from citizens on daily life issues captured the hearts of the citizens. Needless to say, actions taken to adequately please the public were performed within the limits of the city's budgetary framework. I believe that it was not merely the process of coming up with ideas individually, but it was also the suggestions and requests from citizens that inspired further thinking and ideas on how to improve the department's performance. To read the heart of the customer and go one step further in providing the service that is expected reflects true customer service.

Inspiration in Sales: It is an extremely dangerous endeavor to act upon or execute sales without possessing faith or conviction. This phenomenon can often occur in companies which are overseen or managed by the owner, resulting in countless examples of firms going bankrupt. This is similar to the venture companies which were launched on an inspiration but were destined to vanish in the blink of an eye. It goes to show that an endeavor which lacks conviction is dangerous. Recently a newspaper was hailed as a 200 year old company. It is the undeniable result of a consistent succession of leaders who

いたら後先を考えずに実行に移したがる行動力抜群の典型的なナイスガイであった。ビジネス会議では、よく「待て！」の指示を受けていた。思い出した機会に、彼の面白い思いつきが引き起こした笑えぬ混乱に触れたい。彼はバイクが大好きで、休暇の折にはよくバイクツーリングを楽しんでいた。京都付近で落車し、京都市内のある有名病院に入院した。骨折しただけで健康であるから、病院食だけでは当然満足できない。思いついたのがピザの宅配である。最初は、病院も大目に見ていたが、他の患者が真似しだし、ピザの配達が盛んになり、病院の食事システムが混乱してしまった。病院から大目玉を食い、早めに追い出された（退院させられた？）。実話である。今頃、ニューヨークでどうしているのやら。

　また、最近話題のB.A氏。彼の「思いついたら実行する」の基準は、税率である。氏は北フランスに生まれ、フランスのナポレオンが開いた理工系エリート校であるエコール・ポリテクニクを卒業し、ファミリービジネスに入り、今やエレガンスの象徴といわれるモエ・ヘネシー・ルイヴィトン（LVMH）のオーナーである。傘下にはクリスチャン・ディオール、ルイ・ヴィトン等があり、フランスはもとよりヨーロッパ有数の資産家である。フランスが社会党政権になって税率が上がることになり、1981年に米国に移り、米国籍をとった。政権が変わると1984年にはフランスに戻りフランス国籍となった。2012年、フランスに再び社会党政権ができ、年収100万ユーロ超の個人には最高75％の税を課すことが発表されると、突然9月に、ベルギーに移ることを公にした。この信念たるやお見事。物静かで話し方は穏やかだが、ビジネスは非情を超えて無慈悲とも、カシミヤをまとった狼ともいわれる。ベルギー政府は資産家にして投資家が来てくれるなら大歓迎だという。一方、フランスでは、先進国では類を見ない75％という高税率に対し、新政権の支持率は早くも急落している。

respectively managed the newspaper with a sense of responsibility and conviction.

Let me share an experience I had several decades ago. It involved an American friend of mine, Mr. M.M., who had come to Japan while employed by a foreign firm as a section chief in marketing. He was a wonderfully nice guy who was an outstanding man of action. If he had an idea or inspiration, he would, without thinking of here and after, immediately go into action. It was not unusual for him to be told "Wait!" in business conferences. What made me remember him was an episode which resulted from one of his funny inspirations which turned into a disruption that could not be laughed away. He loved to motorbike. Whenever he had a holiday or vacation, he would enjoy touring on his motorbike. Unfortunately one day he had an accident near Kyoto, and was taken to a rather famous hospital located in Kyoto city. Aside from suffering a fracture, he was healthy. Naturally, the food served in the hospital did not satisfy his appetite. To solve this, he had the bright idea of ordering pizza and having it delivered to his hospital room. At first, the hospital looked the other way. However, other patients started to copy the practice of ordering pizza, which resulted in disrupting the hospital's food service system. The hospital was furious, and undertook the process of an early discharge of M.M. from its facilities (or was it time for his discharge anyway?). This is a true story. I wonder what he is up to now in New York.

Let me turn to a fairly famous individual, Mr. B. A. The foundation of his 'Act upon Inspiration' is the rate of taxation in his native country. He was born in northern France. After graduating from the famous elite culinary institution established by Napoleon, the École Polytechnique, he joined the family business. He is now the owner of the recognized symbol of elegance Moet Hennessey Louis Vuitton (LVMH). Affiliated businesses include Christian Dior and Louis Vuitton, among others. Needless to say, he is one of the wealthiest individuals of not only France but of Europe as well. When France's Socialist Party came to power, the rate of taxation was increased. Thus, in 1981 he moved to the United States and became a citizen. In 1984,

when France experienced a change in government rule, he returned to France and changed his nationality to become a French citizen again. This year (2012), France again has a Socialist government ruling over the nation. The government announced that an individual with an annual income of over one million Euros would be taxed a maximum rate of 75%. In September Mr. B.A. suddenly let it be known that he would be moving to Belgium. You cannot but admire this tremendous conviction. He is known for his soft spoken demeanor and quiet attitude toward matters. However, once the matters become business, he is said to be both ruthless and merciless. There are those who refer to him as a wolf wearing cashmere. As for Belgium, they welcomed the arrival of not only an extremely wealthy individual, but an investor as well. On the other hand, France, which now taxes at an unprecedented rate of 75% upon its wealthy citizens, is already showing a sharp decline in support toward the new government.

第5話
強い使命感を持て

　「使命感を持て」とは、難しいことではない。それぞれの立場で、自らの責任を明確にして実行に移し、他人(ヒト)に評価をしてもらうということである。すなわち、〈自らの立ち位置で→自らの責任を明確化し→自ら実行し→他人による評価を受け→自らの価値の創出をする〉。価値の大小は問わない。他人のためになれば、それで良いのである。

　1980年代、米国中西部のある町で、X.W氏はホテルのシングルルームを無料で与えられて住んでいた。顔立ちは立派で身長は2メートル超、ネイビーブルーのセーラーキャップをかぶった姿は、映画『007』シリーズに出てくるかと思う程であった。精神的に少し病んでいたが、何をしていたかというと、ドアマンの傍らに立ち、用心棒といった風情であった。行事があると人捌(さば)きを手伝う。市民の集いのリーダーも家に招いて茶菓を共にしていた。私が着くと銃規制の集まりに連れて行ってくれたり、ゴルフの傘をプレゼントしたりと、不思議なフレンドシップをお互い楽しんでいた。大相撲の本(英文)を土産にすると、喜んで皆に見せてまわっていた。彼の生み出した価値は小さいかもしれないが、皆に愛され彼なりの使命(使命感としては、多分気づいていないであろう)を果たしたのだと思っている。今は世を去ったが、時々懐かしく思い出している。

Number Five
Possess a Sense of Mission

It is not difficult to 'Possess a Sense of Mission'. Within a company, that sense of mission can be implemented by 1) understanding one's position within an organization, 2) clearly perceiving and clarifying one's responsibilities, 3) acting upon one's responsibilities, and 4) being evaluated by others.

In short, looking from where you stand, one step leads to the next: → clarify your own responsibilities → initiate your own actions → be evaluated by others → create your own value. It is not whether your value is large or small. If it benefits others, this is what counts.

In the 1980s, Mr. X. W. was living free of charge in a small single room of a hotel located in the mid-west of the United States. He was a handsome man who stood over 6 feet tall. When he wore a navy blue sailor's cap, at first glance you would think he came out of a recent 007 James Bond film. He suffered from a slight psychological disorder, and I would often wonder what he did for a living. He came across as the man who stands next to a doorman to provide security. If there was an event at the hotel, he would be there to help and to make sure people were lined up and things were in order. He would be invited to have tea at the local citizen's group leader's house. When I arrived he offered to take me to a gathering on gun restriction, and gave me a golf umbrella as a gift. We mutually enjoyed an odd friendship. I once gave him a Sumo wrestling book (in English), at which he was overjoyed. He showed it to everyone he came across. Perhaps the value he generated may have been small, however his mission or sense of mission was to be loved by those around him. While others may not have recognized his mission as such, it

米国製薬大手のフランク・デニソン氏（Frank Denison）は、対日政策のエグゼクティブとして、少し気の短いところはあるが、使命感の非常に強い人であった。その使命の1つとしてA社奨学金を設立した。日本の若い創薬科学者を毎年1人選び、A社で講演の後、好きな研究機関を訪問する約10日間の旅費・宿泊費を提供する制度であった。1980年代という時代、このような制度はアカデミアでは評価され、日米関係のために多くの価値を創出した。しかし、もう1つの使命である日本製薬会社との合弁事業の発展については、研究開発関連の条件が日本の規制の国際化の進展とともに、彼の会社にとって不利となった。その責任を追及され、誇り高く独立心の強いテキサス男（Texan!）デニソン氏は、会社を辞した。

　デニソン氏はのちに、やはり中西部の大手企業アップジョン社に礼をもって迎えられた。新天地でも日本における前社の人脈を生かし、アップジョン社の新たな使命を、強い使命感を持って実行していった。おこがましいが、筆者がアップジョン社に移ったのもデニソン氏がきっかけである。当時米国本社から来ていたU.アクセン氏が中心になり、日本の基礎科学者を表彰する制度として創設されたアップジョン社科学賞もデニソン氏の前社における成果の継続である。デニソン氏も今では故人となり、アップジョン社の名もM&Aで消えたアップジョン社科学賞も、筆者がイーライリリー社に移って10年で終わった。しかし、デニソン氏のパッションと使命感の強さを、友人として今でも誇りに思っている。時は移り、人は変わっても、このような使命感の強い素晴らしい人は、日米欧を問わず数多くいるものである。論より証拠、成功者が後を絶たずに生まれてくるのだから。

　一方で、使命を与えられても、使命感を自覚せず、いたずらにヒト・

had its effect. Although he has passed away, at times I find myself remembering him with fond memories.

Dr. F. Denison. represented one of America's major pharmaceutical manufacturers as an executive responsible for policies toward Japan. Though he had a temper a little on the short side, he was a man with a very strong sense of mission. One of his missions was to establish a scholarship in the name of 'A' company. The scholarship was to be awarded once a year to a young drug discovery scientist, who, after a speech at 'A' company, would be given an honorarium to pay for travel and accommodation expenses to visit a research facility of his/her choice for 10 days. During the 1980s this type of system was valued by those in academia, which in turn generated significant value for U.S.-Japan relations. However, another of his missions was the progress of a joint venture project with a Japanese pharmaceutical company. The international development of Japan's policy toward research and development resulted in a disadvantage for his company. When questioned about his responsibility, this proud man, who was much the independent spirited Texan, resigned.

Later Dr. Denison. was welcomed to another mid-western major pharmaceutical company, The 'U' Company. Even in his new environment, he made use of the network he had built in Japan while employed by his previous firm. With his new responsibilities for 'U' Company, he proceeded to take action to fulfill his sense of mission. It was through Dr. Denison that I joined 'U' Company. At the time, Dr. U. A., who had come to Japan from the U.S. head quarters, and establisher an award to honor Japanese basic scientists. The 'U' Company Science Award was an effort to sustain the results obtained by Dr. Denison while at his former company. He has since passed away, and the 'U' Company name has also vanished through a M&A deal. The 'U' Company Science Award was discontinued when I moved on to 'EL' company 10 years later. However, as a friend, I am still proud of Dr. Denison's passion and strong sense of mission. Although time goes by and people change; I have found that there are many wonderful individuals who possess a strong

カネ・モノを浪費する困った人も存在する。成果は出ない。だから使命感を持てというのである。明確な使命を受けて日本に送られても、保身のためならパワーハラスメントも何のそのという輩(やから)も少なくない。

F.デニソン博士・メアリー夫人と（1987年）

sense of mission regardless as to whether it is in Japan, America, or Europe. Seeing is believing, and the evidence is in the fact that successful individuals are being born without end.

On the other hand, there are those unfortunate individuals who possess a mission, but do not awaken to the sense of mission. This results in people, money, and resources being totally wasted. There is no outcome. This is why it is essential to possess a sense of mission. Although sent to Japan with a clearly defined mission, it is not rare that there are some pathetic individuals who instead resort to power harassment as a method for saving one's skin.

第6話

コンプライアンス遵守の徹底

　コンプライアンスという言葉を私が最初に聞いたのは、1980年代のアップジョン社における"Code of Conduct（行動指針）"である。表紙が緑色でグリーンブックと呼ばれていた。リリー社に移っても赤色の表紙の"Guidelines of Company Policy（会社方針のガイドライン）"というレッドブックがあった。毎年1月1日付でサインをしていたのを記憶している。もちろん、全社員にその方針が説明される研修があり、出席は義務付けられていた。

　このような、組織内における行動指針を見ていると、どうも個人としての生き様（子供の、青少年の、夫婦の、祖父母の、従業員の、等）のコンプライアンスが守られることが重要である気がする。そうはいっても、組織としてコンプライアンスが守られないことが多いので、コンプライアンス違反が新聞種になる。コンプライアンスには個々人の使命（与えられた仕事）とそれを実行する手段・工程も含まれることを自覚していないケースが見受けられる。

　米国医薬産業において、CEOが2代続いて突然の辞任発表となったトップ企業がある。CEOのH.M氏が2006年に辞任し、次のCEOのJ.K氏も2010年12月に突然辞任となった。業績（売上）は世界トップを走り続けているのに、なぜ（why）なのか？　会社の価値（value）である株価が

Number Six
Loyalty to Compliance

The first time I heard the word 'compliance' was in 1980 as part of U Company's "Code of Conduct". The "Code of Conduct" was a book that had a green cover, resulting in it being referred to as the Green Book. When I joined E. Lilly Company, there was a red-covered book entitled "Guidelines of Company Policy," also known as the Red Book. If I remember correctly, every year shortly after January 1st signatures were collected. Of course there were briefing sessions, to which attendance was compulsory. The meetings were for all employees to ensure that the Company's position was explained and relayed thoroughly.

When reflecting upon an organization's code of conduct, I've come to believe that within the multitude of aspects of the code, at each phase of an individual's way of life —as a child, as a young man/woman, as a married couple, as a grandparent, as an employee, etc.— there is an importance that compliance is honored. This being said, all too frequently we learn of breaches in organizational compliance. These offenses become the source for widespread negative newspaper coverage. Looking into the cause of these breaches, in many cases it can be said that there is a lack of conscious awareness toward one's mission (the job or work allocated), and the methods taken to execute this mission.

Within the pharmaceutical industry of the United States, there is a company that had to deal with announcing the sudden resignation of two consecutive CEOs. CEO Mr. H. M. resigned in 2006, and the succeeding CEO Mr. J. K. abruptly resigned in December of 2010. Corporate performance as mea-

3分の1以下になったためである。会社の価値 (value) としての株価が上昇することこそが彼等のコンプライアンス・使命だったにもかかわらず、見かけの価値である売上を維持するためにM&Aに焦点をあて構造改革を怠ったため、資金を使う買い手の価値（株価）は下がりっぱなしだったのだ。2010年12月、前CEO・J.K氏辞任の日に就任した新CEO・I.R氏は、英国人で化学工学士にして公認会計士だ。不採算部門の整理と自社株買いを実行し、株価は持ち直している。成功を祈りたい。

なお、オバマ大統領の再選が決まり、米国におけるコンプライアンスはますます厳しくなるであろう。オバマ氏が2011年1月に発表したヴォルカー・ルール（Volker Rulle：所有権の移動、投機筋への投資など銀行が大きなリスクを負うような投資の禁止）が、実行されるであろうから。2008年に破綻したリーマン・ブラザースの教訓からである。リーマン・ブラザースは、もとはドイツからのユダヤ系移民であったリーマン家（レーマン）の3兄弟が1850年に創業した名門会社で、米国4位の巨大な銀行・証券会社であった。この二足の草鞋（わらじ）で、貸付債権が証券化されたサブプライム・ローンに手をつけて大やけど。まさにヴォルカー・ルールの裏を行ってしまった。チャプター・イレブン (Chapter 11) を申請したが却下され、万事休す。公的資金の注入を受けたゴールドマン・サックスやシティグループに比べると気の毒な気もするが、手段が悪質だったのである。創業家にどう顔向けできるのか。

一方、日本でも、度重なるコンプライアンス違反を繰り返し、一般紙にまで取り上げられて、恥をさらしている財閥系の会社がある。記者会見では業績自慢を繰り返しているが、日本はコンプライアンス違反についての罰則はとても甘いので、コンプライアンス違反の重要さがわからない。米国に倣え（なら）とは言わないが、CEOが捨て身で舵を切れば、会社

sured by sales was impressive, continuing to reflect the Company's position as global leader. Then why the sudden resignations? The company's stock value had dropped to one-third of its previous value. Although it is the CEO's compliance or mission to ensure that the company's value (stock price) continues to rise, these two CEOs disregarded structural reorganization, and instead placed their emphasis on continuing M&A deals that reflected a 'no-basis' value to the company. This resulted in a consistent decline in stock prices/value of the firm. In December 2010, on the day that former CEO Mr. J. K. resigned, Mr. I. R., a British gentleman who was not only a chemical engineer but also a certified public accountant, was named the new CEO. Through the liquidation of non-profitable divisions, as well as purchasing the company's own stock, he has brought about a recovery in the stock price and value of the company. I continue to pray for their success.

In addition, with the re-election of President Obama, focus upon compliance in the United States is going to increase in severity. In January 2010, President Obama publicly endorsed the Volcker Rule (restricting banks and other financial institutions from taking part in proprietary trading risks that do not benefit their clients). Legislation has since been passed to amend this rule. These actions were lessons learned from the 2008 collapse of Lehman Brothers. Lehman Brothers was founded in 1850 by the three Lehman brothers of Jewish immigrants from Germany. The firm became one of the finest in the financial sector, ranking as the fourth largest banking and brokerage institution in the United States. However, when it started to actively deal in subprime loans, it got badly burned. What they did was the opposite of what the Volcker Rule was restricting. Although Lehman Brothers applied for Chapter 11, this was denied, and they had no way out. When compared with Goldman Sachs and the Citigroup, which received public funding in a bailout, there may be room for some sympathy for Lehman. However, we have to recall that their methods were unscrupulous. How are they going to face the founding family?

On the other hand, in Japan, there have been repeated compliance of-

全体へのインパクトは絶大であり、全社員が身震いしてコンプライアンス遵守に進むであろう。釈迦に説法か？

(Green Book)

The Upjohn Company

Cold of Corporate Conduct

Corporate Compliance Program

(Red Book)

Eli Lilly and Company

Guidelines of Company Policy

---

fenses shamelessly made by a 'zaibatsu'-related company, which were even covered by major newspapers. At press conferences this company continues to boast of their performance. This strange phenomenon is able to occur because the Japanese are extremely passive toward compliance offenses. There is total lack of understanding of the gravity of compliance offenses. I am not saying that Japan should fall in line with the United States, but if a CEO is willing to risk everything and take firm control at the helm, the resulting impact to the company is enormous. All those employed by the company will tremble and proceed with their responsibilities while honoring the compliances set by the firm. Is this "Preaching to the choir"?

第7話

「エンパシー」の心を身につけよ

　"sympathy"は日本では同情と訳される。他人(ヒト)と同じ気持ちになるということだ。中国では可憐、同情とも書く。

　Sympathyに似た英語で"empathy"という言葉がある。これは相手・他人の気持ちになって考えるという言葉で、一言で訳せる日本語が筆者には思い当たらない。真の友人には、同情だけではなれない。相手・他人が成功するか失敗するかにかかわらず、相手の気持ちになって考えるということは、生身の人間としてはそう簡単ではない。

　しかし、東日本大震災でみせた日本人のボランティア活動は、empathyの心そのものであった。日米関係についても、両国の官民一体となっての"友達作戦(TOMODACHI)"は大成功し、empathyの一例として特筆すべきことである。

　私事でおこがましいが、海外で宗教を問わず(ユダヤ、キリスト、イスラムなど)、訪ねれば気軽に泊めてくれる友人がいる。皆、筆者の良し悪しを含めて理解してくれている(と思っている)。特に失敗については、原因を一緒に真剣に考えてくれる。

　日本人は同情心の強い国民性である。最近、筆者は駅でコートを忘れ

Number Seven
Possess "Empathy"

The emotion of 'sympathy' is interpreted in Japanese as [Doh Jyo] and its definition is of course the same as in English: sharing the same feelings as another individual especially in sorrow and anguish; reflecting pity and compassion.

The English word 'empathy' has a similar meaning to 'sympathy'. The word 'empathy' in short means to place yourself in someone else's shoes, which can help in understanding what they are thinking, and how they are feeling. For me, being Japanese, I cannot think of a single word in Japanese to properly express this meaning. True friendship cannot be based on sympathy alone. It would not be an easy task for a person to truly understand another individual's feelings resulting from their success or failure.

However, it was evident that it was with empathy that the Japanese volunteers responded to the Great East Japan Earthquake, which was a 9.0 magnitude earthquake that occurred on March 11, 2011 off the Pacific coast of Oshika Peninsula of Tohoku, Japan. It was the fifth most powerful earthquake in the world since modern record keeping began in 1900, and resulted in thousands of deaths, injuries, and missing people, and in US$235 billion in damages (World Bank estimate). It should be especially noted that within U.S./Japan relations, a similar reflection of empathy was seen in operation TOMODACHI, an extremely successful disaster response project which was a unified effort by the public and private sectors of both countries mobilized in response to this disaster.

I must confess with humility that I have the great fortune of having

たが、困るであろう見知らぬ相手のことを考えてか、きちんと届けられていた (empathy)。また最近、筆者の友人 (香港在住のインド系) が洋服の入った手提げ袋を地下鉄丸ノ内線の駅のベンチに置き忘れて、電話をしてきたことがあった。「日本人はempathyだから、君が困っているのではないかと考えて届けてくれるはずだ」と言うと、「駅には日本人ばかりでないからなぁー」と嘆いていたが、次の日にはちゃんと届いていた。日本人に拾われて良かったとは、変なオチである。

　このようにempathyな日本人であるが、時に、競争相手の成功に対しては、個人的に複雑な対応になるケースもある。相手の気持ちになって心から祝福する気持ち (empathy) を持ちたいものである。競争相手の失敗に対してもそうだ。政界の大物I.K氏が、1965年7月8日に急逝した折、「K先生は、お隠れになりました」と言って失笑を買ったT.T氏がいたが、反対派の中には「ソレ、赤飯だ！」と言った人がいたという話を聞いたことがある。情けない話である。

　ここで、最近話題のempathyの実話に触れたい。ダイアナ妃の盗聴 (ハッキング) 等、コンプライアンス問題で話題の世界のメディア王、ルパート・マードック (Rupert Murdoch) であるが、その母親であるデーム・エリザベス・マードック (Dame Elisabeth Murdoch) が、最近103歳で亡くなった。彼女は社交界デビューした18歳で、42歳にして独身の富豪サー・キース卿 (Sir Keith Murdoch) に見初められ結婚。ルパートと3人の娘に恵まれ、生まれ故郷のメルボルン近郊の豪邸で生涯を過ごした。しかし、息子のビジネス上のコンプライアンスに対しては、スタッフがやったことであっても訴訟などするものではない、また、プライベートな離婚・再婚に関しても、自分は賛成できないと、都度メディアに公言するなど、世界のメディア王となった息子に諫言を怠らなかった。オー

friends abroad who, regardless of their religion (Jewish, Christian, Muslim), easily allow me to spend the night in their homes. They all are aware, and accept (I believe), my virtues and vices. Especially regarding mistakes, they earnestly make the effort with me to think of what may be the cause.

The Japanese, as a people, have a strong sense of empathy. Recently, I had forgotten my coat at a train station. By perceiving the emotions that the person who had lost his/her coat would be experiencing, someone had made an effort to deliver my coat to the station master's office. Again, a friend of mine, Indian by decent who was living in Hong Kong, recently called me saying that he had forgotten a bag which contained his clothing on a station bench of the Marunouchi subway line. I told him that because the Japanese possess empathy, someone would surely find the bag and, by perceiving his predicament, would hand it over to the proper authorities. His response was only to lament that all he could see around him were Japanese people. However, the following day the bag was, as I had predicted, delivered. It is a rather strange way to put it, but he was lucky that it was a Japanese person who picked up his forgotten bag.

Although in general the Japanese possess a strong sense of empathy, at times when a rival or competitor succeeds, an individual may experience complicated emotions. It would be gratifying to possess empathy and perceive what the individual must be feeling, and be able to congratulate him/her from the bottom of one's heart. This should be the same even when one's rival or competitor experiences failure. Mr. I.K., an influential political figure, suddenly passed away on July 8, 1965. It is said that, upon hearing that Mr. I.K. had passed away, a member of a rival faction said, "Bring out the Red Rice." (In Japan red rice is traditionally served at celebrations). This is a pitiful example.

I will like to touch upon a true story involving empathy. The media mogul Rupert Murdoch recently had to answer for methods toward compliance employed by his staff, such as wire-tapping Princess Diana's phone, among other offenses. His mother, Dame Elisabeth Murdoch, recently passed away

ストラリアでは、偉大な慈善家として社会への貢献で有名な超一流の女性であった。1970年代には、女王陛下の名代である総督（Governor General）に推薦されたが、固辞したと言われる。ご冥福をお祈りしたい。

アンカラ大学（トルコ）QSRI研究室、イズマイル・ヤルツェン教授兼アンカラ大学副学長夫妻（前列右端）、トウバ・ボレリ講師（前列左端）と研究スタッフ（2012年）

at the age of 103. She made her social debut at the age of 18, and was spotted by the wealthy Sir Keith Murdoch, who at the age of 42 was still single. The two married and were blessed with three daughters and Rupert. Dame Murdoch lived in a mansion located just outside of Melbourne, which was where she was born and ultimately spent her entire life. However, regarding her son's attitude toward business compliance, she said that although a member of the staff may be responsible, legal action should not be taken against the staff member. She also said that she did not agree with covering private matters such as divorces and re-marriages in the media. She seemed to take every opportunity to scold the actions of her son, the global media mogul. In Australia she was an extremely renowned philanthropist, making generous social contributions. She was a truly great woman. In 1970 she was nominated for the honorary position of Governor General, which she declined. I pray that she rests in peace.

Together with friends of Ankara University (2012)

第8話
どう違う——見るとå<ruby>相</ruby>る

　"見る"という文字は、目の下に2本の足がある。人の目線で他人(ヒト)を見るということである。人の目線で話すことはempathy（参照：第2章第7話）の心でもある。"相"という字は、目の左に木を書く。木の上に立って見るということである（鳥瞰図）。

　相るということで、私は最近面白い話を聞く機会があった。数年前に私のオフィスを訪ねたことのある若手建築家K.T氏（著名な建築家である安藤忠雄氏の門下）が、また訪ねてくることになった。彼は約束の時間に現れた。「電話があってから、迎えに出る心算であったのに。よくわかったね」と言うと、「一度来たところは迷わず行けます」と言う。地図を見ただけで行くところに必ず行けるという。鳥瞰図ならぬ、地図・図面の上を歩いているのだという。一流の建築家の感覚の鋭さに感心しきりであった。また、何年か前にテレビで見たが、日本人最初のF1ドライバー中島悟氏は、信号で止まった時に四方を見廻すと、その時見た風景が鳥瞰図になるという。出発に向けて心・身共に準備完了なのである。これがプロフェッショナルといわれる人の感覚なのかと感心したものである。

　世界の一流といわれる人には、何かこのような"人の目線で話せる心(empathy)"と"木の上に立って見る、話せる心(oversee)"が備わってい

Number Eight

The Difference between Seeing and Viewing

Those of you who are familiar with the Japanese language (written and spoken) will easily understand that many words, although phonetically similar, have very distinct and different meanings. An example is the character '見る' [to see], which is represented by a combination of the character for the eye [目] and placing two legs under it. The meaning of this new character is to see at another individual's eye level, which is similar to the concept of empathy, referred to in narrative Number Seven. Another character which can also be pronounced as 'miru' is the character '相', which is a combination of the character for eye [目] with the character for tree [木] written on its left. Thus it means to view from the trees, i.e., looking down, which is similar to 'a bird's eye view'.

In relation to the latter character [相], I would like to relate two interesting stories. A few years back, a young architect, Mr. K. T., who at the time was an apprentice under the renowned architect Tadao Ando, had visited my office. He was scheduled to come see me again. It was approaching the time that was agreed upon for his visit. My intentions were to go out and meet him after receiving a phone call to inform me that he was in the vicinity. However, I discovered that he had found his way to my office. I told him, "I am surprised you found your way." In response, he said, "If I have been there once, I will always find my way without getting lost." He explained that it was similar to having a bird's eye view, and compared it to possessing the ability to walk while visualizing a map or blueprint. I was thoroughly impressed by the acuteness and sense of perception exhibited by this fine architect. In addition,

るような感じがする。しかもその使い分けができる人たちである。2つの心を使い分けられることが大切だと述べたが、人の目線で他人を見ることも、その立ち位置により、随分違ってくる。たとえば、会社の経営者が従業員と語る時には、特に人の目線で話さなくてはならない。これがempathyの心である。一方、経営方針の決定において、従業員の目線で考えていたら、"素早いタイミングで正しい決断（right timing for right decision）"を下せない。それでは経営者失格である。

2012年11月26日、英国財務相ジョージ・オズボーン氏（George Osborne）が英国中央銀行総裁に外国人（カナダ）であるマーク・カーニー氏（Mark Carney、47歳、現カナダ中銀総裁）を任命すると発表した。現総裁の任期が切れる2013年7月に就任の予定だ。破格の給与の提示と（現総裁のほぼ倍額）と三顧の礼によって実現したこの外国人登用は、英中銀創設以来318年の歴史上初めての出来事である。しかしこれは同時に、窒息しかねない状況の英国経済に外部の新鮮な空気を入れることにもなった。市場は直ちに反応した。多くのバンカーたちが賛同すると共に、英国内においても祝福された選抜であったようである。英国前財務相によると、氏はG8やG20においても何が間違っていたのか、何をすべきかを的確に把握していたという。氏のプロファイルを見ると、民間企業での経験、特にゴールドマン・サックスにおける氏のマネージメントスタイルが魅力だったようである。すなわち、時に人の目線で見ること、そして相ることを適宜に切り替えることのできる人なのである。

皮肉なことに、この切り替えで今最も悩んでいるのが、米国大統領オバマ氏と下院議長のベイナー氏であろう。財政の崖（Fiscal Cliff）をめぐり、ともに2つの目線を切り替えることができない状況である。いずれは、いずれかに偏った形で決着せざるを得ないと思うけれども。日本も

a few years ago I was watching the first Japanese F1 driver, Satoru Nakajima, on television. He was saying that when he stopped at a signal and looked around in four directions, his vision would become a bird's eye view. This meant that just before starting, the preparation of his mind and body were complete. Again, I was impressed with the perception of the senses of this individual, who was referred to as a professional in his field.

I cannot help but deduce that those who are first class, or fine examples of their respective professions, possess the ability to view events at another's eye level (empathy), and the ability to stand on top of a tree and look down or oversee occurrences. In addition, they possess the capability to understand which to utilize depending upon the situation, a capability that is very important, as previously mentioned. When seeing another individual, depending upon the position or stance of the individual, a great difference can develop between the two methods of seeing. For example, if a corporate executive is talking to an employee, special care must be taken to speak at eye level. This reflects a sense of empathy. On the other hand, for decisions involving the company's direction, the eye level of one employee cannot be considered. If it is, the proper timing will probably be lost and the proper decisions will not be made. This would result in the corporate executive losing his/her position.

Last year on November 26th, the Rt. Hon. George Osborne, Chancellor of the Exchequer of the British Treasury, announced that he was appointing Canadian Mark Carney (Governor of the Bank of Canada, age 47) to the post of Governor of the Bank of England. Mr. Carney is scheduled to be officially appointed after the current Governor's term ends, which will be in July of this year. He will receive an impressive salary (almost twice that of the current Governor) and an extremely sensitive and courteous welcome. This is the first time in the 318 year history of the Bank of England that a foreigner has been appointed to the position of its Governor. At the same time, this appointment will bring in fresh air from the outside to the almost choking English economy. The market immediately reacted. Many bankers were in favor of the appointment, and within England in general, the people blessed his can-

政権が変わったが、日本の政界は世界三流と言われないためにも、2つの目線の切り替えを適宜に的確に願いたいものである。

didacy to the position. According to the previous Chancellor of the Exchequer, Mr. Carney at the G8/G20 summit perceived precisely what was wrong with the British economy, and what had to be done to correct it. From reviewing his profile, it can be noted that his experience in the private sector, especially his management style at Goldman Sachs, is attractive. In short, he possesses the capability to view events at another's eye level, and the capability to perceive and take on a bird's eye view of events.

It is rather ironic that there are two other individuals who have yet to master when to use one method of seeing versus the other. They are United States President Obama, a Democrat, and Speaker of the House of Representatives John Boehner, a Republican. While facing the 'fiscal cliff' and being from opposing political parties, they were both incapable of viewing events using the proper method. One side will ultimately lean toward the views of the other, which is what I believe is probably the way the budget battles will be settled. In Japan, to avoid Japan's politics from being referred to as third rate in the world, I sincerely hope that the current political leaders possess the capability to utilize the two ways of viewing matters with precision and appropriateness.

第9話

近いうちに──定量的か定性的か

　2012年8月、当時の与党民主党・野田佳彦総理は、野党自民党・谷垣禎一総裁に衆議院解散を迫られ、「近いうちに」と答えた。結果として、11月16日解散、12月26日が総選挙になったため、この"近いうちに"は3〜4カ月ということになった。近いうちにとは何カ月かという議論がメディアを賑わした。次の参議院選までの4年近くであると言う人も出たくらいである。しかしこれで、日本では近いうちにと政治家が言うと、まあ3〜4カ月を意味することになるだろう。

　米国では、連邦政府が"a few"と言うと数字の2または3を指し、"several"と言うと数字の4ないし5を指すのが標準である。すなわち、政府がa few daysと言うと2〜3日を指し、several monthsと言うと4〜5カ月を指すということになり、かなり定量的に予測することができる。もちろん、共和制である米国に解散はないが。

　日本では、先ほども触れたが、政界で近いうちにと言うと、3〜4カ月と定量化されるだろう。野田総理は実行したのだから。民主党はそうだったが、自民党は違うということはあるまい。

　近いという言葉は、時間・距離・人間関係などではかなり定量的である。「すぐ近くですヨ」と言われると、5〜6分で行けるかなと思う。「近

Number Nine

'In the Near Future', is This Quantitative or Qualitative?

In August of 2012, Japan's administration was held by the Democratic Party of Japan. Prime Minister Yoshihiko NODA was being pressed by the opposition leader, Liberal Democratic Party (LDP) President Sadakazu TANIGAKI, as to when a decision would be made on the dissolution of the Lower House, which would immediately lead to elections. Prime Minister Noda responded, 'In the near future.' Ultimately the dissolution occurred on November 16th and general elections were held on December 26th. Thus, 'the near future' was 3 to 4 months. The timeframe represented by 'the near future' was a theme of heated debate within the Japanese media. At one point, someone even said that it meant at the time of the next Upper House elections which were, at that time, a year away. However with the aforementioned turn of events, now we have a rough idea that in Japan when a politician says 'in the near future', you can assume it means 3 to 4 months.

In the United States, when the national government mentions 'a few,' this indicates 2 or 3. When the term 'several' is used, it means 4 to 5. It is good that there is an established benchmark. Thus when the government says 'a few days,' this means 2 to 3 days, and if it says 'several months,' it indicates 4 to 5 months. This provides a quantitative prediction of the expected timeframe. Of course, because the U.S. is a Republic, it does not have dissolutions. However, these terms are used in other political discussions.

In Japan, as aforementioned, political circles have established that 'in the near future' in the quantitative form means 3 to 4 months. Prime Minister Noda has now established a precedent. If the Democratic Party has shown

い親戚です」となると、いとこくらいかと考える。

　しかし、これが「近いうちに」となると、かなり定量的に判断するのは難しい。あいさつ代わりにも聞こえる。それでは、前述の野田総理は、あいさつ代わりに言ったのかというと、それはない。総理という公人として言ったのだし、実際に解散を実行した。

　さて中国では、「近いうちに」というのは、どのくらいを意味するのだろうか。友人に聞いたところ、どうも日本語の漢字とは、感覚が違うようである。中国語の"近日"というのは確かな数字を意味するらしく、中国語の"最近"というのは日本語の近いうちにと近いような感じがするという。

　英国の友人によると、英国首相の任期は5年と決まっており、解散風が吹くこともないという。現英国首相キャメロン氏の任期は2015年。5年かけて周到に準備をする。しかし、5年が近づくとメディアが動き出すという。"in the near future"というと、大体3～4カ月を指すが、"soon"となると、さらに近くなるという。

　2013年1月22日（火）という日時をめぐって、英国とEUの間で双方に驚きと困惑が発生した。最近、英キャメロン首相は、英国のEUメンバーシップについて、EU内でビッグトークを行う発言をしていた。そして、突然ドイツで1月22日（火）にそれを行うと発表。驚いたのは、独首相メルケル女史と仏首相オランド氏である。2人は6カ月前から、第2次大戦後の独仏和解のシンボルであるエリゼ協定の締結50周年記念を、ドイツでこの1月22日（火）に行うと決めていたのである。英キャメロン首相は、蚊帳の外。びっくりした独メルケル首相より連絡があり、

that 3 to 4 months is 'the near future', it would be hard to imagine the Liberal Democratic Party having a different interpretation.

The word 'near' is a quantitative term which can express time, distance, and relationships. 'It is very near' suggests that it will only take 5 to 6 minutes to reach a specific destination. 'A near (close) relative' suggests perhaps a cousin.

However, when it comes to the term 'in the near future,' it is sometimes quite difficult to make a quantitative decision. It comes across as a greeting. Well, does that mean that the aforementioned Prime Minister Noda used this term as a greeting? No, that could not be the case. He used the term in his official capacity, and he did as he stated. He executed the dissolution of the Lower House within 3 to 4 months.

Out of curiosity, I wondered what 'in the near future' would mean in China. I learned after making an inquiry to a friend that the Chinese express it with different characters from the Japanese kanji. The Chinese characters used for 'near future' have an established number attached to their meaning. What the Chinese reflect in writing as 'recently' would be close to what the Japanese would write as 'in the near future'.

According to an English friend of mine, the term of office for the British Prime Minister is established as 5 years, so there is no potential of a dissolution wind to blow in. The term of the current British Prime Minister, David Cameron, will conclude in 2015. Knowing that the term of office is 5 years allows meticulous preparations to be made for his successor. However, as the 5th year nears, the media will start to go into action. 'In the near future' roughly indicates 3 to 4 months. However, when it comes to the term 'soon', the timeframe becomes closer.

Events that were planned for Tuesday, January 22nd of this year caused surprise and confusion in both the U.K. and Germany. Recently, Britain's Prime Minister Cameron stated that high-level talks would take place in the European Union (E.U.) regarding the U.K.'s membership to the E.U. Then suddenly an announcement was made that the talks would take place in Ger-

英キャメロン首相は日時を1月18日（金）に変更、場所もオランダに移したのである。しかもエリゼ協定は、1946年時の英チャーチル首相が独仏にそろそろ仲よくしたらと言ったことがきっかけという。英独仏はつかず離れず上手くやっている。日米中も知恵を出し合ってほしいと願う。

チャーチル首相

many on January 22nd. This announcement particularly surprised German Chancellor Merkel and French President Hollande. The two leaders had agreed (6 months prior) to commemorate the 50th Anniversary of the Elysée Treaty, a symbol of reconciliation between the two countries, in Germany on January 22nd. British Prime Minister Cameron was the odd one out. The startled Chancellor Merkel made this conflict known to Prime Minister Cameron, who rescheduled the high-level talks to Friday, January 18th and relocated the venue to Holland. Thinking back, it was in 1946 that British Prime Minister Churchill suggested that it was high time that the French and Germans reconciled, which ultimately led to the Elysée Treaty. The British, German, and French are extremely good at keeping a measured distance from one another. I sincerely hope that Japan, the U.S., and China will share in each other's wisdom.

第10話

「遠交近攻」──ボスとの付き合いにどう生かす

　ちょうど30年前の1982年、三菱系社長のS.F氏と、ポーランドの首都ワルシャワのホテルで食事をしていた。興に乗った氏は、"春夏冬中"と書き、「何と読む？」と問う。秋がないのですねと言うと、そうだと言い、"秋ない中"すなわち"商い中"という意味だと教えてくれた。さらに続けて、"遠交近攻"という言葉について解説してくれた。遠くと交わり、近くを攻める。一瞬、洋の東西を問わず、出る杭は打たれ、出る杭を打つものだという現実、いざ勝負となれば、世間は非情なものであるという事を思い出していた。

　上司との関係は、健全なものであることが基本だ（a healthy relationship with the boss）。だから往々にして、上司との良好な関係を維持発展させることに時間とエネルギーをかけないことが多い。まあ、日本には"ノミニケーション（飲む＋コミュニケーション）"という言葉があるくらいなので、欧米に比して問題は少ないのかもしれない。

　上司との健全な関係を築くには、どうしたらよいのか。まず、①上司に課せられている最終の数値目標を理解し、そこから来る上司のプレッシャーを理解するべきである。そして、その強みと弱みを把握し、上司の仕事のスタイル（参照：第2章第1話）を理解することである。次いで、②自己分析である。自らの能力（強みと弱み）を把握し、特に自分が上司

Number Ten

'Interact with Those Who are Distant, Antagonize Those Who are Near'
——How to Utilize This When Interacting the Boss

It was exactly 30 years ago in 1982 that I was having a meal with Mr. S.F., a president of a Mitsubishi group firm, in a hotel located in Warsaw, the capital of Poland. He was beginning to warm up and starting to relax when he wrote 'In spring, summer, winter' in Japanese characters. I inquired "How do you read that?" His response was "There is no autumn." In Japanese, "Aki nai Chu" phonetically means 'in the process of doing business.' It is a form of a word game in which Japanese characters which represent an unrelated object or subject convey a meaning phonetically. Mr. S.F. continued to write a different set of characters, of which he provided an explanation. He said "Interact with those who are distant, and antagonize with those who are near.' In an instant I recognized that, regardless of eastern or western societies, the reality is that the stake that is poking out will be hammered back in. I remembered that the moment a competition begins, the battle can easily become merciless.

In business a healthy relationship with the boss is fundamental. However, people seldom spend the time and energy necessary to sustain and build a favorable relationship with their bosses. Well, here in Japan there is a regular practice of 'drink coms,' which are opportunities to communicate while drinking at local establishments after work. Thus, compared with western culture, perhaps the problem may be less relevant in Japan.

How does one go about building a healthy relationship with their boss or superior? There are several steps that one can take. ① Understand the final numbers and outcomes that your superior has to ultimately achieve, and perceive the pressure he/she is under. In addition, recognize your boss's strengths,

に頼りたがるような性格なのか、それとも上司と距離を置きたがる性格なのか（後ほど筆者の体験を述べたい）を知ることが大切である。

　以上の2点を踏まえて築いた上司との良好な関係を維持するため努力をする必要がある。すなわち、③上司も忙しいので、手短に肝心なことを報告することが大切である（right timingでright thingsを報告する）。効率のよいスタッフとは、このような者をいうのであり、上司も自ずと目をかけてくれるはずである。

　筆者は、今まで多くの欧米人・日本人のスタッフに助けられてきた。どこでも、上司を頼りに伸びていく人、上司から距離を置いて伸びていく人がいる。私は前者には綱を短くして、こちらから話しかけるようにし、後者には綱を緩め、危険域を超える前にグッと引っ張るようにした。泣きながら食ってかかる者もいたが、ジックリと自らの仕事の役割を話せば、わかるものである。懐かしい思い出である。

　さて、遠交近攻に戻ろう。上司の上司から直接声がかかった場合、そのやり取りに透明性があれば問題はない。たとえば、直属の上司にも話があって、声をかけてくれたとか。そうでない場合は、直属の上司への忠誠心も問われよう。すなわち、飛び越えて声がかかりましたと上司に報告するのか、黙って会うのか。直属の上司について、前述の①、②、③を試してみたが物足りないと自ら判断したならば、覚悟の上でその上の人間に会うことをすすめる。近くを攻めることはしなくても、遠くと交わるのはよい、と私は思う。

　また、組織外の方々と交わるのは、非常に大切なことである。例えば人材会社から声がかかるのは、楽しいもので大切にすべきである。これ

weaknesses, and work style (refer to Insight Track Number One). ② Conduct a self-analysis. Recognize your own capabilities and weaknesses. It is particularly important to know if you are the type who depends on your boss, or if you are the type who distances yourself from your boss (I will later share an experience). It is necessary to strive to sustain a good working relationship with your boss. This can be accomplished through utilizing these two methods. Thus, ③ your boss is a busy individual so it is important to remember that when reporting to your boss, there is a proper time and proper method for your interactions. The proper method may be through a meeting, a phone call, a formal memo, or an Email, depending on the nature, complexity, and urgency of the issue. A staff member who is efficient in this respect will inevitably be recognized by their superiors.

    I, myself, have been on the receiving end of support and assistance by many western and Japanese staff. I must mention here that there are those who develop through depending upon their superiors, and there are those who develop through distancing themselves from their superiors. In my case, when interacting with an individual who fit in the first category, I kept the leash short and proactively took the initiative to talk with this individual. When interacting with an individual who fell into the second category, I kept the leash long and loose, but just before this individual crossed into a dangerous zone, I gave the leash a quick firm tug. Of course there were occasions when an individual would retaliate while crying, but all it took to resolve this was a good long talk on what this person's professional role was. This all brings back good memories.

    Let me return to the theme of 'interact with those who are distant, and antagonize with those who are near'. There are instances where you directly communicate with your boss's boss. For example, you may be spoken to simply because he/she wished to convey something to your immediate boss. In these cases, if transparency is established, there would be no issue or problem. If this is not the case, your loyalty toward your immediate boss may be ques-

も遠交の恵みである。

　筆者の場合は、よくトップから、または外部から声をかけられることが多く、直属の上司とは非常に上手くいく時と極端に悪い時があった。不徳なのか？

tioned. In short, it is whether you openly inform your immediate boss that his/her superior had approached you, or if you meet with your boss's boss and not say a word. Regarding your superior, if you personally feel that you may have short comings in the previously mentioned ①, ② and ③, I would suggest that you be prepared when meeting with him/her. It is not really necessary to antagonize those who are near, for I believe that it would be far better to approach those who are distant.

I would like to add that it is very valuable to associate with individuals who are outside of your company or organization. Receiving an approach from a head-hunting firm is interesting, and should be valued. I believe that this can also be viewed as being approached by those who are distant.

I am fortunate to frequently interact with top-level individuals, as well as those who are outside of my particular circle. Through these interactions, I have found that there is an extreme difference between those who are very skilled at communicating with their immediate superiors, and those who are not. Is this due to a lack of virtue?

第11話
チームの協力体制づくり

　聖徳太子の憲法一七条(604年)以来、日本は和(なごやか、おだやか『広辞苑』)が中心の社会といわれている。米国では個人中心といわれる。文化としては、この様な表現もうなずける。

　しかし"チームの協力体制づくり（Building Team Cooperation）"では、全く逆である。第二次世界大戦終結（1945年）以来、世界のどこかで戦闘をしてきた米国にとっては、チーム協力体制づくりは不可欠であり、また世界一の手段を持っているのは事実である。最前線では、最小単位のチームの協力体制が整っていなければ戦えない。一般のチーム協力体制づくりには、種々の方法があり、それぞれに有意義と思われる。

　筆者が体験したチームづくり"チームの生産性を上げる"を述べてみたい。まず、生産性を上げる提案をして、周囲の反応が良くなかった時でも、「駄目だ」と言うことは禁句である。提案のよい点を誉めて、「こういう案はどうですか？」と自らの提案を説明する。次にチームメートの失敗を人前(チーム会議)で責めないことである。その人からの、あなた自身への信頼を失うからである。これは大きい負の点数取得である。私の実体験であるが、リーダーを執拗に責め続ける男をリーダーが黙って部屋から連れ出し、部屋の鍵を閉めて会議が再開となった。これは凄いと思ったものだ。さらに連れ出したのも、連れ出されたのも、ユダヤ系で

Number Eleven
Building a Team Cooperation Structure
—Listening To Opponents

Ever since the year 604, when the Seventeen-article constitution authored by Prince Sh?toku was introduced, Japanese social values have been said to be centered on harmony. In the United States, it is the individual's dignity and rights that are protected by its Constitution. When generally referring to cultural aspects, it is relatively easy to understand that this kind of phrasing would be appropriate.

However when it comes to building team cooperation, it is totally different. Since the end of World War II (1945), for the United States, which has been fighting battles all over the world, building team cooperation is an absolute necessity, and in fact they do possess the highest level of methods to do so. At the frontlines, battles cannot be fought without an established team cooperation structure even within the smallest possible unit. In Japan, the direction to which a team will proceed is ultimately led by the individual who talks the loudest during the meeting. This frequently results in comments such as "That guy's attitude is unbelievable" after the meeting. However, in a multi-national corporation, this process is unacceptable. In a meeting or discussion environment, a timeframe or limit is sometimes set to allow an individual to present what is on his/her mind, but to prevent rambling and doodling. Other than this, the debates often have no boundaries. When a decision is made, all are to honor and proceed with this decision. Those who are unable to accept and honor the decision will ultimately leave the team or the firm. In Japan, globalized organizations follow the same process.

Here I would like to share, from my own experience, how a team's pro-

あったので、その根性を見る思いをしたのも事実である。このリーダーは後程、業界で大成功する一人になった。連れ出された男は、かつて私にレポートした時期があった。目前に2人の顔が浮かぶようである。

　もう1つ申し上げたいのは、議論が行き詰まった時、このチームの目標達成に相応しい"一語（a one-word）"を考えてみるのも楽しい。「～を男にしよう！」「お客様は、神様ではない。神様はわたし（ぼく）です！」などなど。これは、チーム全員が賛成しないとできないことで、たまには息を抜くのも悪くない。

　さて冒頭に戻って、聖徳太子であるが、当時の朝廷と豪族（蘇我氏、物部氏など）との血で血を洗う乱の数々から、太子は和のない当時の日本を憂えて「和を以て貴しとなす」を憲法十七条の基本にしたのである。奈良、平安、安土桃山、そして江戸、現代と、和の文化は見事に花開いたが、源平、鎌倉、室町、信長・秀吉の戦国時代は、和の世界とはほど遠い。太子は多神教である仏教（多神教の神道と矛盾しない）をもとに、この国に和をもたらそうとしたが、2人の風雲児（清盛は比叡山に弓を引き、キリシタンを保護した信長は延暦寺他を焼き打ちにした）が現れた。結果として、家康が江戸幕府の安定運営のため、仏寺の保護と共に太子の和を日本に定着させたような気がする。秀吉・家康による多くの名刹が今に残る。

ductivity increases through building the team itself. Let us say someone offers a proposal to increase productivity. Even if the reaction of others on the team is not all that positive toward this proposal, to voice "No way!" is not allowed. It would be important to praise and focus on the positive elements of the proposal, and to provide suggestions or ideas in a collegial manner such as asking "How about this idea?" You can then start the process of explaining your alternate proposal. In doing so, you will find that those around you will see you as a leader. Next, when a team member has made a mistake, it is important that you do not openly scold the individual at a team meeting, even if he/she may be a regular offender. If you do so, you will lose this individual's trust. This will result in your accumulation of negative points. From my own personal experience, there was a man who continually berated the leader during meetings. The leader just seemed to have had enough, and physically took this man outside the door, slammed it shut, and locked it. At the time I thought "Wow". The leader who took the individual physically out of the room and the individual who was taken out of the room were both Jewish Americans, which to me, strongly reflected the Jewish spirit, or their sheer guts. This leader later went to work for another company, and became hugely successful within the pharmaceutical industry. The individual who was forcefully taken out of the room, at one time was reporting to me. I can recall both of them vividly.

There is one more thing I would like to convey, and that is when discussions have run into a dead-end, it is beneficial and good for the morale of the team to start thinking about an appropriate word or sentence that ties in with the team's goal or objective. Some examples include "Let's make ----- a man" or "The customer is not the Almighty? I (or he/she) is Almighty." This action requires the entire team's approval to accomplish, but at times it is necessary to relieve the tension and get the creative process started again.

Returning to the time of Prince Shōtoku, this period in Japanese history was noted for the frequent and constant battles between the Imperial court and powerful ruling clans (e.g., Soga and Monobe). It was through these

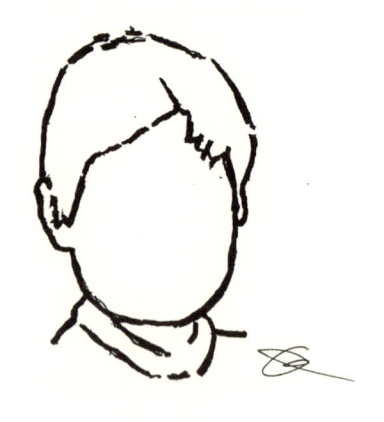

bloody and numerous conflicts that the Prince came to view with dismal foreboding the status of the country. He realized that there was, at the time, a lack of harmony in Japan. Thus, he made the principles of "Harmony is to be valued, and the avoidance of wanton opposition is to be honored" as the foundation of his Seventeen-article constitution. The cultural principle of harmony bloomed magnificently during the Nara, Heian, Azuchimomoyama, and Edo periods, as well as during the present. However, during the Genpei, Kamakura and Muromachi periods, in addition to during the reigns of rulers such as Nobunaga and Hideyoshi who were major figures in the Sengoku period (Warring States period), a total distancing from the principle of harmony was seen. Although the Prince had endeavored to bring about harmony to this country through the polytheistic religion of Buddhism, historical figures such as Kiyomori, who had challenged Hiezan (Enryaku Temple), and Nobunaga, the war lord who defended Christians, torched Enryaku Temple. I have a feeling that these actions resulted in Ieyasu's strategy to preserve temples and establish the Prince's principle of harmony to try to ensure the stable management of the Edo Shogunate (government). Today, there remain numerous great temples built by Hideyoshi and Ieyasu.

第12話

キャリア女性のキューピッド
――魂の通い合うパートナーを探せ

　バークリー・インターナショナル（BI：Berkeley International）という会社を聞いたことがおありだろうか。メーリッド・モロイ女史（Mairead Molloy）が設立したロンドンに拠点を置くマッチ・メーキング会社である。事業所は他に南イングランド、スコットランド、オーストラリア、ベルギー、ニューヨークと最近開設されたパリにある。完璧なパートナーを探し当てる――見つけにくいものを見つける（discern）――能力を備えた組織である。究極の目的は、"魂の通うパートナー（soul-mating)"を探すことであるという。

　ヨーロッパ事業をモロイ女史と合弁で立ち上げ、その運営を仕切るインガ・ヴァビーク女史（Inga Verbeeck）をめぐる記事を、最近のフィナンシャル・タイムズ（FT：Financial Times）のヒュー・カーネギー記者（Hugh Carnegy）の記事で読み、BIの存在を知ったという次第である。ヴァビーク女史について少々触れたい。彼女は、父親創立のスチール貿易会社（アントワープ）のCEOであったが、米国の投資会社に売却の後、長年コンサルタントとして友人であったモロイ女史と意気投合して、そのヨーロッパ事業を、特にキャリア女性のキューピッドになるべく引き受けたという情熱の人である。女性エグゼクティブは独立心も高く、強いけれども、それはそれ、強く生活力のある男性に惹かれるという女性本能は消えないものだという。

Number Twelve

A Career Woman's Cupid

Have you ever heard of a firm by the name of Berkeley International (BI)? It is a match-making company that was established by Ms. Mairead Molloy. The firm's headquarters is based in London, and it has offices in southern England, Scotland, Australia, Belgium, and New York. It recently launched an office in Paris. The organization is noted for its capabilities in searching and locating the perfect partner for its discerning clients, even when that partner is elusive. Its ultimate goal is to locate a "soul-mate" partner for its clients.

Ms. Inga Verbeeck established a joint venture with Ms. Molloy, and oversees the management of its European operations. I learned of the existence of BI through a recent article in the Financial Times, written by Hugh Carnegy. Allow me to touch upon a little background of Ms. Verbeeck. Her father was the CEO of a steel exporting company (Antwerp), which was bought by a U.S. private equity firm. After this, she caught up with her friend Ms. Molloy, who was a long-time consultant. Upon learning of BI's business, Ms. Verbeeck decided to become responsible for its European operations. She particularly wanted to become a career woman's cupid, which reflected her passionate character. Women executives are known to be extremely independent and strong, which seems to reflect the way things are. However, they often are still attracted to men who have the financially capability to sustain a particular lifestyle or family. That is, they are attracted to men who are as capable as they themselves are.

It has been ten years since BI was established, and it currently has a membership of 3,000 (their goal is 10,000). Their objective is to match globe-trot-

BIは、創立10年でメンバーが3000人（目標は1万人）になり、世界を飛び回るエグゼクティブのマッチ・メーキングをするのだという。しかもマッチングが成功したカップルのフォローアップサービスをする仕組みもある。コストは年間1000ユーロから5000ユーロとケースバイケースである。3000人のメンバーの60％は女性であり、そのうち約60％は離婚経験者で、ヴァビーク女史自身、今は離婚しているが前夫との関係は続いているという。女性メンバーの中に日本人がいるかどうかわからないが、問い合わせてみたいと思っている。面白いことに、女性の相手としては、紳士でありハンサムが多い英国人が"よい相手（a good catch）"だと思うと述べている。イタリア男性は相手を自分の好みに合わせたがるが。日本の女性もこのようなマッチメーカーに登録して凄いカップルが誕生すればよいと思う。日本で活躍している欧米人で日本語が流暢な方は、日本人が奥様というケースが多い。日本女性は、こんな所に登録しなくても充分に魅力的なのだ。欧米人にとって！　アジア事業でも提案しようかとも思ったが、無理筋であろうか。

　日本でも、少子化対策など政府の政策もあって、婚活が盛んになった。コストもかからず、良心的に効率よく運営されているケースも増えている。例えば、三菱系会社によるダイヤモンド・ファミリー・クラブ。社員の子弟を登録し、希望条件に合ったパートナーを探すというシステムである。人を大切にするいかにも三菱らしいクラブである。また、私の畏友である米川耕一弁護士（参照：第1章第11話）は、フランス料理店（会費制）で口コミによるパートナリングを行っている。当局による独身証明書が条件という公明なものである。多忙で魅力ある女性の皆さまが、真に"魂の通うパートナー"にめぐり合うことを祈りたい。世の常なれど、狼に御注意を。

ting executives. In addition, the firm also has a process which conducts a follow-up service for successfully matched couples. The annual cost ranges from 1,000 to 5,000 Euro, or can be charged a rate on a case-by-case basis. Of the 3,000 members, 60% are women, of which 60% have experienced a divorce. Ms. Verbeeck herself is divorced, although she still sustains a relationship with her former husband. I don't know if any Japanese are part of BI's women members, but I would like to find out. It is rather interesting to learn that the women clients have said they consider Englishmen to be gentlemen, handsome, and a good catch. They believe that Italian men try to mold women into their own tastes. I would really like to see a Japanese woman register as a member of this match-maker company, and observe a fantastic couple develop. The majority of westerners who reside in Japan and are extremely fluent in Japanese, are married to Japanese women. I believe that Japanese women are attractive enough (perhaps for Westerners!), and would fare well even without registering for this type of service. Maybe I should propose that the firm consider launching operations in Asia, but this may be a little far-fetched.

In Japan, with its shrinking population, the government is pursuing policies to tackle the low birth rate. With this backdrop, so called 'spouse hunting' activities have become popular. There is an increase in low-cost, reasonable, effectively managed cases. For instance, there is the Mitsubishi-related company's 'Diamond Family Club'. The way the system works is that employees' children register and supply their specific desired conditions. A partner who matches these requirements is then searched out. This club reflects the very essence of Mitsubishi because both value people. A respected friend and lawyer, Mr. Kohichi Yonekawa (refer to narrative No. 10 of Ten Commandments of Becoming an Internationally Minded Person, Sept. 12, 2011), has been holding partnering dinners at a French restaurant (requiring membership) on a word-of-mouth basis. According to the authorities, regulations require proof of being single be presented in order to attend, making it extremely clear and fair. I sincerely pray that those women who are busy and attractive find their true 'soul-mate' partner. However, as the saying goes, they must "Beware of wolves."

第13話

女性エグゼクティブが時代を変える

　ニューヨークや東京の証券取引所が株価指数を出しているように、ロンドン証券取引所（LSE：London Stock Exchange）も子会社であるFTSEから100種総合株価指数（医薬品は3社）などを取引のある日に必ず出している。その100種会社の取締役会（Boardroom）に女性が少ないのを嘆き、デーヴィス卿（Lord Davies）が、2015年には女性の割合を25％まで引き上げるべきだという報告書を出している（2011年）。しかし、2012年11月でもいまだ17.3％だという。

　期せずして、日本の安倍首相が少なくとも会社1社あたり少なくとも1人の女性エグゼクティブを配することを目標にしてほしいと述べた記事がフィナンシャルタイムズの週末版（FT Weekend、2013年4月20日）に掲載された（Jonathan Soble：ジョナサン・ソーブル記者）。

　筆者の関連する医療関連分野では、オバマ政権における米国保健福祉省の長官がキャサリーン・セーベリュウス女史（Kathleen Sebelius）であり、FDAもマーガレット・ハンバーグ女史（Margaret Hamburg）、FDA-CDER（医薬評価機構）のトップもかの有名なジャネット・ウッドコック女史（Janet Woodcock）であり、女性エグゼクティブの花盛りである。さらに、同じく官では、今日本で話題の元米国通商代表部代表のカーラ・ヒルズ女史（Carla Hills）がいる。

Number Thirteen
Executive Women Change Generation

Similar to the New York and Tokyo stock exchanges, which put out stock price indexes, the FTSE, a subsidiary of the London Stock Exchange (LSE), is responsible for 100 different corporate stocks (including 3 pharmaceutical firms). In the event that there is trading in these stocks, which occurs on a daily basis, they are required to announce the stock price indexes. Distressed that of these 100 firms very few women were on the Boards, and concerned about the slow rate of addressing this issue, the UK Government pledged to "promote gender equality on the Boards of listed companies" (Coalition Government Agreement). Edward Davey, the Business Minister, and Lynne Featherstone, the Minister for Women, invited Lord Davies of Abersoch to lead a review of the current situation. Lord Davies, in 2011, published the 'Women on Boards' report, which advised that the number of women on Boards should be increased to 25% by 2015. However, this number was only at 17.3% in November 2012.

By chance, in an article of the Financial Times weekend edition written by Jonathan Soble, Japanese Prime Minister Abe was quoted as saying that the goal is to have at least one female executive in each firm (FT/Weekend/April 20, 2013).

In the healthcare segment, a field which I myself am a part of, there are numerous extremely capable women in the Obama Administration. These include Kathleen Sebelius, Secretary of the Department of Health and Human Services; Margaret Hamburg, Commissioner of the Food and Drug Administration (FDA); and Janet Woodcock, the Director of FDA-Center for Drug

また、民間のペプシ（PepsiCo）では、インド生まれのインデラ・ヌーィ女史（Indra Nooyi）が2006年以来、会長兼CEOである。そのキャリアたるや、驚くべきものである。インドのマドラス・クリスチャン・カレッジで化学、物理、数学を修め、インドにおいてMBAを取得し、ジョンソン＆ジョンソンのプロダクトマネージャーなどを経て、米国イェール大学でMBAを取得。その後はボストン・コンサルティング、モトローラを経て、1994年にPepsiCo入社となる。2001年に財務担当責任者（Chief Financial Officer）、そして2006年にはトップに上り詰め、現在に至る。取締役会13人中、女性は彼女を含めて4人（31％）で、妥当な数字である。社内執行役員26人中、女性は7人（27％）で、10人集まれば3人女性であり、まあこれも妥当かと思う。インデラ女史のような女性が、日本から生まれることを期待したいものである。

　米国では、他にも大手企業で女性CEOが数多く活躍している例があり、ヒューレット・パッカード社のメグ・ホイットマン（Meg Whitman）などが挙げられる。アジアで活躍している女性エグゼクティブでは、フィリピンのテレシタ・シー・コソン（Teresita Sy-Coson：小売業トップ）がおり、中国福建省出身で、インディラ（Indra）と同様に移民国で活躍している。

　一方、製薬企業はどうかというと、執行役員にはそれなりに女性エグゼクティブが30％前後いるが、CEOとなると皆無である。例えば、イーライリリー（Eli Lilly）では取締役会の女性比率は29％（14人中4人）、執行役員会も29％（同じく14人中4人）である。ファイザー（Pfizer）では、取締役会が、29％（14人中4人）、執行役員会では、31％（13人中4人）である。

Evaluation and Research (CDER). In addition, there is a previous leading officer of the US government, who is well known in Japan, Carla A. Hills, former U.S. Trade Representative.

Looking at the private sector, India born Indra Nooyi has been the Chairman & CEO of PepsiCo since 2006. This lady's career is amazing. After majoring in chemistry, physics and mathematics at India's Madras Christian College, she joined Johnson & Johnson to become their product manager. She studied at Yale University in the U.S. and earned an MBA. She experienced a period at the Boston Consulting Group prior to joining Motorola, and in 1994 became employed by PepsiCo. In 2001, she became the firm's CFO, and in 2006 she climbed to the top of the firm, the position she holds today. On the PepsiCo Board there are 13 executives, of which 4 (including Indra) are female (31%), a respectable number. Of the firm's 26 corporate officers, 7 are female (27%). Thus, in the event 10 executives meet, 3 would be female, again a respectable number. I hope for the day that we will see a woman like Indra emerge in Japan.

In the United States, there are many examples of large corporations which are managed by female CEOs. A good example would be Meg Whitman of Hewlett-Packard. In Asia, Teresita Sy-Coson, who is in retail, was originally from China's Fujian Province, and later moved to the Philippines. Similar to Indra, she became successful and active in a country to which she immigrated.

On the other hand, within pharmaceutical corporations female executives represent approximately 30%. However, when it comes to a CEO, so far, none have been appointed. For example, at Eli Lilly the ratio of female to male executive board members is 29% (4 out of 14), and the ratio of corporate officers is the same, 29% (4 out of 14). At Pfizer, female to male executive board members are at a ratio of 29% (4 out of 14), while the corporate officer ratio is 31% (4 out of 13). Taking a look at these figures, it becomes pretty clear that when comparing the representation of women executives between the U.K. and the U.S., the ratio is lower in the U.K. compared to that of the

このような数字をみると、米国に比べ英国の数字は低く、デーヴィス卿が女性エグゼクティブを増やすよう発破をかけたのもうなずける。

　ところで、なぜ大手製薬企業には女性CEOがいないのだろうか。医薬事業は、トップ自らが現場主義(walking manager)を務めないと何も決められないほどに深化し、多様化している。某CEOなどは、中国訪問の折、北京の中央政府だけではなく各省の省都をめぐる数週間の出張をこなしている。製薬業界では、どのような能力がCEOにとって必要であるかが明確でない。現在のCEOは、医師、科学者、経済学者、弁護士、公認会計士など、その背景は多様している。従って女性対男性という視点で議論をするのは慎重を要すると思われる。

United States. It is no wonder Lord Davies introduced the 'Women on Boards' initiative.

Let us reflect on why there are no women CEOs in major pharmaceutical corporations. Within the pharmaceutical industry, the leading executive is often referred to as the 'walking manager' because of the necessity of personally executing a hands-on policy or approach to efficiently respond to and make strategic decisions within a constantly evolving and diversifying industry. For instance, a certain CEO, on a visit to China, not only made a visit to the central government in Beijing, but also visited the main cities of individual provinces, which ultimately extended his business trip by several weeks. Thus, perhaps the reason there are no female CEOs is that pharmaceutical industry has not decided on what capabilities in a CEO are best suited for managing a company in the industry. The CEOs currently represent a variety of backgrounds, including physicians, scientists, attorneys, economists, CPAs, and sales professionals. People with such major differences in background naturally have differences in philosophy as to the best approach for managing the company. As an example, a major company recently changed CEOs from a business person, to an attorney, and finally to a chemical engineer/CPA. So while working out the best qualifications for a CEO, the industry may be wary of adding a different variable into the discussion, that of a male versus a female CEO. (refer to narratives Number 4, 9, and 10 of Ten Commandments of Becoming an Internationally Minded Person, Sept. 12, 2011; and narrative Number 6 of Insight Track),

第14話

コーポレートガバナンス
——スウェーデン・ビジネスモデルとバイキング

　コーポレート・ガバナンスとは、かなりその国の文化や地勢に左右される地域性の高いものである。手前味噌になるが、前章「国際人になるための十戒」の十戒を各個人が守っていれば、組織がコーポレート・ガバナンスを謳わなくても良いのだが。厄介なことに、健全な企業には経営者にも従業員にも事業目標があり、それを満たすためには存分な活動の中にも法的な縛りが必要である。そこに労使の強い絆も生まれるのである。それがコーポレート・ガバナンスである。

　コーポレート・ガバナンスについてビジネスモデルを通して覗いてみたい。米国には典型的なアングロ‐サクソン・モデル（Anglo-Saxon Model）が存在する。投資家（株主）は、その会社の方針（経営者：managements）が気に入らなければ、株を売ってしまうという簡単なものである。大口の投資家やヘッジファンドが株を手放せば買収される前にも倒産である。現在、欧米の金融機関のインサイダー取引、脱税などは見ていられない有様で、連日新聞を賑わしている。一方、知恵を働かしているのはクラフト（KRAFT、米国）を買収したカドベリー（Cadbury、英国）で、英国と米国の課税システムの違いを利用して、違法ではないが税回避に精を出している。

　いずれにしても、会社組織を倫理的に強固なものにすることが肝心で

Number Fourteenth
Corporate Governance
——Swedish Business Model and Vikings

It can be said that corporate governance highly reflects regionalism whichis determined by a nation's culture and geographical characteristics. Allow me to refer to my previous series [Ten Commandments in Becoming an Internationally-Minded Person]. If an individual were to absorb and honor these 'Ten Commandments', there would be no necessity to specifically address corporate governance. Unfortunately, however, there is the desire in every healthy corporation to attain specific goals by both the management and employees. Within the process of attaining these goals to the fullest extent, the necessity of a certain level of legal restrictions becomes evident. This is what brings about a strong bond between management and employees. This is corporate governance.

Let us take a look at a business model to understand corporate governance. In the United States there exists a classic Anglo-Saxon Model. If investors (shareholders) of a company are disappointed in the company or do not like the company's management style or policies, they can simply sell their shares. If a major shareholder or hedge fund decides to sell shares of a company, prior to any acquisition plans, the company can fall into bankruptcy. Currently, in the U.S. the number of cases of insider trading by financial institutions and cases of tax evasion is unbelievable. Every day newspapers are filled with related articles. On the other hand, there are those who skillfully utilize their wisdom to take advantage of tax laws for the benefit of the company. For example, when Cadbury acquired KRAFT, they took advantage of the differences in tax laws between the U.K. and United States, which led to legally

あり、それがコーポレート・ガバナンスでもある。全従業員の徹底した教育・研修が必要である。それには莫大な予算が必要であるが、前述の如く、労使共に個々の教育研修が大切である。幸いにして日本の金融機関は、かつて政府による資金注入はあったが健全である。安倍総理が女性役員を1人は置くように要望したと聞いたが、日本のコーポレート・ガバナンスでもっとも大切なのは、社外取締役の存在である。お忘れなく。

　ところで、現在静かに興味が持たれているスウェーデン・ビジネスモデル (Swedish Business Model) についてはお気づきだろうか。コーポレートパワー（会社の主権）が、マネージメント（経営者）にあるのではなく、シェアホルダー（株主）にある。株主は、取締役の選任はもちろんのこと、重要な政策決定に直接関与する。株式会社であれば当たり前のプロセスで、日本にも株主総会はあるが、日本の株主総会が対立の場であるのに対し、スウェーデンの場合、総会は労使協調の場なのである。人口わずか1000万人の国が、世界的に著名なヴォルヴォ (Volvo) やエリクソン (Ericsson) などを生み出しているのはなぜだろうか。フィナンシャル・タイムズ (Financial Times) のリチャード・ミルネ (Richard Milne) 記者によれば、それは事業発展の基本の長期安定政策にあり、短期的に見ればいただけない方針であっても、長期安定に必要な政策であれば採用するという。会社は永く続かなくては (sustainable) 意味がない。昔、ヴァイキングがリーダーを選ぶ時は、海賊全員の意思（コンセンサス）により知略に富んだ者が選ばれた。腕力だけが強い者ではない。筆者は、このスウェーデンのビジネスモデルはヴァイキングの流れ（文化）だと思っている。

　しかし、カリスマ性の強いCEOをいただく家具のイケア（IKEA）は

avoiding taxation.

Whatever the case, corporate governance is designed to ensure that the company's organization is firmly based upon ethical principles. To accomplish this, comprehensive programs of education and training involving all employees are a necessity, which requires a tremendous budget. As previously mentioned, it is important to conduct specific education and trainingtoward management and labor. Fortunately this appears to have happened in Japan because, although the Japanese financial institutions were injected with public funds which can potentially lead to waste and abuse, they remain healthy. Also, I have heard that Prime Minister Abe has voiced a request that corporations have at least one female member on their Boards. However, it is far more important in securing Japan's corporate governance that Boards contain at least one outside Board member.

On a different note, I wonder if recognition is being made toward the Swedish Business Model which is currently stirring quite a lot of interest. Its characteristic is that management power is not in the hands of the management, but in the hands of the shareholders. Shareholders, needless to say, have the authority to appoint board members, but also to become directly involved in management decisions made regarding important policies. This is a perfectly natural process when we are talking about a joint-stock corporation. In Japan we also have general shareholders meetings; however, these shareholder meetings are often used as venues of confrontation, whereas in Sweden they are opportunities for collaboration between management and labor. Though Sweden is a nation with a population of only 10 million, it has introduced globally recognized manufacturing brands, such as Volvo and Ericsson. How was this accomplished? According to Financial Times journalist, Richard Milne, it was through the basic fundamental business development practice of taking a long-term stability policy. Thus, a strategy that provides only short-term stability may not be accepted, but a strategy that is necessary for long-term stability will be adapted. A company would be meaningless if it is not sustainable on a long-term basis. Long ago, when the Vikings were choosing a

オランダに、そして容器のテトラ・パック（TETRA-PAK）は本社機能をスウェーデンとスイスに分けている。時代の流れか。

　一方、残念ながら、一党支配の中国やロシアにはコーポレート・ガバナンスなど存在すらしていない。

© rimglow - Fotolia.com

leader, they did so through a unified consensus, and ultimately the leader was selected for his abundant knowledge and strategic skills, and not by physical strength. I personally believe that Sweden's business model takes after the Vikings culture.

It is interesting to note that the furniture& home products company IKEA, led by a highly charismatic CEO, is based in Holland, and the container giant TETRA-PAK has divided its headquarters functions to Sweden and Switzerland. On the other hand, unfortunately, corporate governance does not even exist in countries ruled by one-party systems, such as China and Russia.Perhaps it's the changing of times.

第15話
名もなき道を行くなかれ

　表題の「名もなき道を行くなかれ」は、旧制第四高等学校の寮歌の一節「〜名もなき道を行くなかれ、吾等の行手星光る」からの引用である。名もなき道を行くことで迷ってはいけないということである。これは、夏目漱石の小説『三四郎』の中で、三四郎が美禰子に Stray Sheep（迷える子羊：「新約聖書」の一節）と軽く"あしらわれた（cold shoulder）"ことと同じようなものである。すなわち、続く「吾等の行手星光る」の星とは、自らがやりたい・なりたいことである。自らの星を明確にしてこそ、迷わずに到達できるという現代のビジネスにも通ずる言葉である。しかも日本語らしく情緒あふれる言葉である。

　さて、現実のビジネスとして「星」を定め「迷わず」に実行するために機能している米国のシステムについて意識されたことがあるだろうか。特に製薬会社においては、CEOが取締役会会長（Chairman of the board）と会社社長（President of the company）を兼務するシステムである。CEOが退任する時に一時的に会長（Chairman）になり、新CEOが社長（President）を務めるということは往々にして起きる。しかし会長（Chairman）がすべての業務から退任すると、かのCEOは従来の図式を踏襲する。しかし、最近のマイクロソフトでは、創業者ゲイツ氏が会長を続け、CEOのバルマー氏が解任されることになっている。特例か。

Number Fifteenth

Don't Take a Road with No Name

The subject phrase 'Don't Take a Road with No Name' was taken from a segment of the dormitory song of the Fourth High School of the old-education system in Japan which states: '. . . . Don't Take a Road with No Name, Stars will Shine Our Path.' This phrase advises against getting lost, or losing one's direction. Within the famous novel 'San Shi Roh' by SousekiNatsume, this is reflected in the scene where the main character of the novel, San Shi Roh, gets the cold shoulder from Mineko, the young lady he is infatuated with. She compares him to a 'Stray Sheep', which is taken from the New Testament. Further, in the second phrase; 'Stars will Shine Our Path', the 'Star' refers to what an individual wishes to accomplish, and who they aspire to become. Through clearly identifying and perceiving one's 'Star', one can achieve an aspiration or goal without becoming lost. In today's business scene, people can easily relate to this phrase. Particular to Japanese, the phrase expresses an abundance of emotion.

Let us examine the real-world business environment todetermine whether there is an American system which is actively functioning and consciously establishing the 'Star' and progressing without becoming 'Lost'. Particularly in a pharmaceutical company, there exists a system where the CEO concurrently serves as Chairman of the Board and the President of the firm. It is frequently observed that when the CEO retires or resigns, he/she will, for a specific period, serve as Chairman, and the newly appointed succeeding CEO will be the active President of the firm. However, when this Chairman completely steps away from the business, the new CEO will follow the fundamen-

その点、日本では社長が会長になるとすべての執行権をCEOとしての社長に譲り、自らは財界活動に専念することが多い。この財界活動(経団連、商工会議所、同友会など)は、米国の共和制とは違って公式なロビー制度がない日本では意味がある。財界とは、霞ヶ関・永田町に対して、アドバイスとロビー活動をするという意味で独特なシンクタンクであり、重要である。

　その日本において、一時期一般的であった株の持合制(Cross-shareholdings)を、第二次大戦後イタリアで立ち上げた人物についてフィナンシャル・タイムズ(Financial Times)で読む機会があったので触れたい。戦後ミラノにできたメディオバンカ(Mediobanca：民間銀行トップ)の創立者であり、以来40年にわたり君臨した故エンリコ・クッティア(Enrico Cuccia、1907～2000年)の話である。彼は株の持ち合い制(Cross-shareholdings)のシステムを創案し、古きイタリアの資産家がお互いに上手に株を持ち合うようにすることで、欧米資本によるイタリア企業のM&Aに対抗したのである。当時、酷暑のミラノで多くの資産家が海に山に避暑に出かけても、黒いハットをかぶり、スカラ座の近くにある自らの銀行(Mediobanca)をやり過ごし、次のM&Aの仕掛けに没頭しながら歩いていたという。午前のコーヒーブレイクで近くのガレリア・ヴィットロ・エマニェル(Galleria Vittorio Emanuele)に歩を運ぶ時、行き交うビジネスマンたちは傍らによけ、道を空けたという。最近イタリア政財界で(悪)名高いシルヴィオ・ベルルスコーニ(Silvio Berlusconi)さえ新参者扱いされ、メディオバンカ(Mediobanca)の取締役(boards)になるために何年も待たされたのは、よく知られた話である。

　しかし、マリオ・モンテ(Mario Monte)前政権によるイタリアのコーポレートガバナンス規制は世界で最も進んでいるといわれ、メディオ・

tal pattern of concurrently serving as CEO, President and Chairman. There are exceptions, as was seen recently in how the CEO of Microsoft, Steve Ballmer, announced his intentions to retire, but founder Bill Gates will continue to be the active Chairman.

Alternatively, Japan has a different system in this regard. In Japan the usual pattern is that when the President becomes the Chairman of a company, he/she hands over all executive powers to the new President (CEO), and dedicates his/her energy to becoming involved with the financial community. The financial community (e.g., Keidanren, Chamber of Commerce, Business Associations) has a strong purpose and specific role in Japan. Unlike America, the practice of recognized lobbying does not exist. The financial community in Japan interacts with the bureaucratic sector in Kasumigaseki and the politicians of Nagata-choto provide advice and conduct lobbying as a group. It also serves as a distinctive and important think tank.

Within Japan, at one-time it was conventional to have cross-shareholding, and I would like to discuss an article related to this that I read in the Financial Times. It dealt with an individual who started this principle in post-World War II Italy. This article was about the late Enrico Cuccia (1907-2000), who, after the War, founded the Mediobanca in Milano, and for 40 years was at the helm. He introduced the cross-shareholding system, which motivated old established Italian investors to skillfully acquire mutual sharesand kept much of the power with the Italians, thus making it difficult for Western investors to conduct merger & acquisition (M&A) deals on Italian corporations. The article noted that Mr. Cuccia, although it was blistering hot at the time in Milano, and the majority of investors were relaxing in the mountains or by the sea, could be seen wearing a black hat, walking past theMediobanca located near the La Scala, ready to set-up the next M&A deal. It is said that when he would be out on his morning coffee break walking near the Galleria Vittorio Emanuela, local businessmen would make way for this financier. Silvio Berlusconi, who recently has become notoriously famous within Italy's political and financial circles, was treated as a newcomer by Mr.

バンカ（Mediobanca）の現CEOであるアルベルト・ナゲル（Alberto Nagel）はこの株の持ち合い制（Cross-shareholdings）を方向転換しようとしている。このシステムがあっても、イタリア大手企業の買収が起きているからだという。今回は横文字が多くなったが、御容赦を。

Cuccia. It is well known that Mediobancatook many years before allowing him on their Board.

It is interesting to note that during the administration of Mario Monti, who was Prime Minister of Italy from 2011 to 2013, Italy's policy toward corporate governance was said to be one of the most advanced. However, Alberto Nagel, the current CEO of Mediobanca, intends to alter directions toward cross-shareholdings. It is said that this is due to the fact that, although this system exists, large Italian corporations are still being acquired by foreign investors.

Enrico Cuccia (1907-2000)

第16話
瞑想は経営の術なりや

　瞑想というと座禅を思い出し、宗教的なものを感じる。しかし、残念ながら筆者に禅寺での座禅の体験はない。一方、欧米の著名な経営者にとって、瞑想（meditation：英和辞典では瞑想）というのは宗教的ではない。かなり目的的でもある。瞑想という言葉で表現される場合、どうも3つのタイプがあるように思える。

　1つは"目的瞑想（objective meditation）"と言えそうだが、あることを念頭に瞑想をする。欧米人に多いケースである。心を無にして（雑念を払って）、あるいは技術的に言うなら、心をその一点だけにホモジニアスにして決断に導く。もう1つは心身の疲れを癒やす"生理的瞑想（physiological meditation）"であり、さらに目的と生理的の2つを兼ねた"第3の瞑想（objective & physiological meditation）"がある。

　瞑想の時間であるが、多忙な人々であるので、20〜30分位であろう。ある経営者は、1日1回、時間を決めて、一言「何も考えない」と言って瞑想に入ると、顔の筋肉が緩むという。すると気付くのである。自然に、意識という感覚の中で機能する思考や感情などを感じるのである。すなわち、瞑想と意識（経営）は共存しているということになる。これが目的瞑想の典型的な例であろう。

Number Sixteenth

Importance of Meditation in Management

Upon hearing the word 'meditation', many of us will envision the religious practice of Zen sitting meditation. However, unfortunately I have never visited a Zen temple in efforts to experience sitting meditation. On the other hand, for renowned corporate leaders 'meditation' is a non-religious mental exercise with an emphasis on a specific target or goal. When describing 'meditation', it can be divided into the following three types: objective, physiological, and objective & physiological meditation.

In the first type, objective meditation, a specific objective or issue is meditated upon. This type of meditation is largely utilized by people in western societies. It is practiced through purging all worldly thoughts from the mind, or to phrase this technically, attaining a homogeneous concentration toward the one objective at hand, to come to the required decision. The second type is physiological meditation, in which the relief of physical and mental fatigue is sought. Finally, the third type of meditation is the combination of the first and second types of meditation: objective & physiological meditation.

The time allocated for meditating, in view that we are referring to those who are extremely busy and pressed for time, would most likely be approximately 20-30 minutes. One executive is said to meditate once a day, during a specific time established in his schedule. According to this executive, "To think of nothing" begins the process of meditation, and eventually leads to the method of relaxing the facial muscles. As the meditation continues, an understanding develops, and within the sensation of consciousness lie the functions of thought and emotion. In short, it can be said that meditation

振り返ってみると筆者は、この40年、どこの組織にいても20～30分くらいは朝か夕に1人の時間をつくった。それは心身の疲れを癒す生理的瞑想だったような気がする。今、その時々の厳しい環境が思い出されて、ほろ苦い。最近では、時間が許せばこれを毎日30分行うことにしている。睡眠不足気味の筆者には、生理的にも瞑想が必要でもある。瞑想（眠り？）に入れるかどうかはすぐ判断できる。瞼の筋肉が緊張している間は入れない。緊張がとれたと感じた時は、10秒もかからない。筆者の瞑想はそんなもので、楽しい夢も見るし、目を覚ましてホッとするような追い詰められた夢も見る。ただ、マーフィーの法則[注]よろしく、迷った時は、潜在意識に答えを考えておけと命じて瞑想する。目覚めて最初の答えが正解、そして実行に移す。単純なものである。

第3の目的・生理的瞑想は、行う人も多いのではないだろうか。瞑想に慣れた人にとっては、何かホッとする状態になるらしい。朝オフィスに来て、全社の懸案事項を眺めるとパニックになりかねない。静かに瞑想を始めると、人間できることしかできないという気持ちになり、仕事の優先順位を素早くつけられるようになるという。とにかく瞑想を日課としている経営者が現実に多いことに驚く。特に危機（crisis:世界中いたるところで直面している）の時にこそ、瞑想を。部下は、あなたの明確な方針を求めて、あなたをジッと見ている。

日本ではアップルの新型iPhoneが発売され大騒ぎである。iPhoneを1日何時間か切って、瞑想してはいかがだろうか。

最近、筆者は幹細胞研究に関する仕事を通して、新たに米国に何人かの素晴らしい友人ができた。特にアサーシス（Athersys）社のCEO、GVB氏とVP、MM女史である。共にいつ寝ているのかと思うほど多忙

and consciousness 'management' coexist. This is a perfect example of 'objective meditation'.

Looking back over the past 40 years, regardless of the organization I belonged to, I took 20-30 minutes of solitary time in the morning or evening. I believe that my meditation was physiological, to relieve mental and physical fatigue. Currently, as I recall the days when my environment was tough, I have many bittersweet memories. Recently, whenever time permits, I try to conduct this meditation every day for 30 minutes. For one who is constantly suffering from a lack of sleep, it is a physiological necessity. It is easy to determine whether I can go into a meditative 'sleep?' state. While the eyelid muscles are tense, it is impossible to meditate. When this tension is relieved, it does not take even 10 seconds. This sums up my meditation method. I have pleasant dreams, as well as dreams in which I feel driven into a corner, and awake with a sense of relief. However, let's not forget the following advice: when in doubt, dictate to your subconscious to come up with an answer, and then meditate. The first answer that comes to mind upon awakening is the right one, to be immediately placed into action. It is a very simple matter.

The third process is objective & physiological meditation. There are probably quite a number of individuals who conduct this. Those who are used to meditation state that it provides them with a sense of relief. Arriving at the office in the morning, and viewing the pending issues of the entire company may bring on a panic attack. Quietly going into meditation will introduce the recognition that there are limitations on what can be accomplished, or rather, immediately provide an understanding of the order of priority. It is surprising to learn that there are many practical executives who routinely practice meditation. Especially in times of crisis 'which confronts the world over', meditate. The people who work for you are all intently staring at you for a clear and precise decision or answer, and meditation can help you reach the best decision possible.

In Japan, Apple launched its new model iPhone, which caused quite a buzz. I have to wonder whether it would be possible and advantageous to

で、目的瞑想とそれを実現するための行動を24時間繰り返しているような感じである。これこそ生き馬の目を抜く米国バイオベンチャーの見本だ。ただ、ファミリーライフとビジネスの区別は明確である。成功を祈ってやまない。

（注）Dr. Joseph Murphy Ph.D.による 'The Power of Your Subconscious Mind'（あなたの潜在意識の力を生かせ：筆者訳）

瞑想——無なりや／有なりや

perhaps turn off the iPhone for several hours a day and meditate. Recently, through taking on a project involving stem cell research, I had the wonderful opportunity to build new friendships with several marvelous American people. In particular, as I came to know a corporate CEO, Mr. GVB, and Ms. MM, a Vice President, I began to wonder, "When do these people ever sleep?" I feel as though they are constantly revolving between objective meditation and taking actions toward realization of their goals, 24 hours a day. It is an example of the cut-throat environment of America's biotech venture business. I must note with some relief that these individuals are able to maintain a clear divide between family life and business. I cannot help but pray for their success.

Rodin "The Thinker" © Brad Pict - Fotolia.com

第17話

脈々と続く同族会社に学ぶ 1
――真のカスタマーは誰ですか

　欧米の大手同族会社では、金融界のロスチャイルド（Rothchild）、ファッション界の新興モエ・ヘネシー・ルイ・ヴィトン（LVMH）、ITのアップルや、マイクロソフト、食品業界のネスレ（Nestle）、医薬品業界の独メルク（Merck AG：米メルクの本家）、メディア界のニュースコープ（News Cope）などを、その経営者のカリスマ性とあいまって興味深く眺めてきた。

　共通しているのは、当然であるが①成功している、②トップ（CEO）は同族から出ている、③その信念・主義主張は決して揺るぎない、という3点である。

　本話では、創業者存命の会社を除き、4～5代または100～150年は続いている同族会社について述べたい。これらの会社に共通するのは、(a) 人を大切にする保守的経営であるが、合理性追求は徹底している、そして、(b) 博愛主義 (philanthropic) に基づく莫大な寄附を行っている、である。

　まず、大きな同族会社であるロスチャイルド（参照：第1章第18話）。創業者メイヤー・アムシェル・ロスチャイルド（Meyer Amschel Rothschild）の5男であるジェームス（Baron James Rothschild）から4男の

Number Seventeenth

The Survival Capability of Family Controlled Companies (Part 1)
——Who are Your Customers

There are numerous examples of western family controlled major corporations; Rothschild of the financial sector, LVMH of the fashion industry, Microsoft the IT industry, Nestle the food industry, and the pharmaceutical industry's German Merck (U.S. Merck's parent firm), as well as News Cope of the media industry. In addition to the charismatic person of their respective corporate managers, it is with great interest that we view these corporate giants.

Looking at what they have in common; (1) obviously, they are successful, (2) the CEO is related to the family and (3) their mantra, principles and policies never waver.

Within this text, excluding companies where the founder is alive, a look into family controlled corporations that are in their 4th or 5th generation, and have existed for 100 to 150 years. The common factors of these firms are; (a) although a conservative style of management in which people are valued, there is a relentless pursuit toward rationality. (b)enormous endowments made, or charitable causes that are based upon the principle of philanthropy.

Firstly, a look at the large family controlled corporation of Rothschild. (refer to number 18 of the Ten Commandments series, April 23, 2012,) Baron James' the France-based Rothschild, who was founder Mayer Amschel Rothschild's 5th son, and it is David de Rothschild, the 4th generation from James, through his formidable ability combined the UK based Rothschild, established by founder Mayer's second son Nathen Mayer Rothschild, which was headed by Jacob Rothschild (Lord Rothschild), with the France based Roth-

デービッド・デ・ロスチャイルド（David de Rothschild）は、その辣腕で知られる。創業者の次男ネーサン（Nathen Mayer Rothschild）が創始した英国ロスチャイルドの現当主・ジーコブ（Jacob RothschildまたはLord Rothschild）が率いる英国ロスチャイルドを統合して"パリ＋英国"ロスチャイルドの当主となった。

一敗地にまみれたジーコブは、息子ナット（Nat Rothchild）を先頭に巻き返しを図っている。英国ロスチャイルドには、ナットをはじめ甥たちが英国独立路線の後継者として控えていると豪語している。また、今までパリ・ロスチャイルド家と米国カリフォルニアのモンダヴィー家との合弁（最初の製品は1981年のオパースワン）以外、金融拠点のなかった米国に英国ロスチャイルド家が拠点を作ることに成功した。米国の名門ロックフェラー財閥（非ユダヤ系）の7代目デービッド・ロックフェラーからその株式37%を買い取りロックチャイルド"Rochchild"ユニットを創設したのである。このような同族会社の中での切磋琢磨がリーダーを育てるのだ。

両家ともその寄付行為は莫大で、年間数百億円単位の慈善事業を世界各地で展開している。現在、東京大学ではそのロックフェラー図書館の改築作業が始まっている。地下40メートルに300万冊の書庫を作るという。このロックフェラー図書館こそ、関東大震災の翌年の大正13年に、当時の400万円（現価格で約100億円）という寄付をロックフェラー財団からいただいて4年後の昭和3年に完成したものである。新図書館は、学内だけでなく学外にも開放し広く活用されるという。

さて私が本当に書きたかったのは、このような巨艦ではなく、どちらかというと小さいが脈々と続いている同族会社についてである。これら

schild and become its head.

The blow that was experienced by Jocob has introduced a resumed offensive lead by his son Nat Rothschild, with his upbringing in the staunchly independent UK Rothschild, is expressing that he is the rightful successor. Apart from the joint venture by the French Rothschild and California's Mondavi family (Opus One winery of 1981), the UK Rothschild were successful in establishing a base within the American financial sector. Rothschild has also bought 37% of the distinguished American Rockefeller family (non-Semitic) shares from the 7th generation, David Rockefeller, to establish a "Rochchild" unit.It is through this type of competition within family controlled corporations, that cultivates leaders.

Both families are known for the enormity of contributions to charitable causes, which annually may go into the hundreds of millions of dollars, going into various charity projects in regions across the globe. Currently, at Tokyo University, the Rockefeller Library is undergoing renovations. Forty meters underground a book vault with the storage capacity of 3,000,000 volumes will be built. It is this Rockefeller Library that was established the following year of the Great Kanto Earthquake (1923), at the time the cost was 4,000,000 Yen (currently it would amount to 10,000,000,000 Yen) and the entirety of this sum was from the charity of the Rockefeller Foundation. Four years later in it was completed in 1928. The new library was not limited to students and faculty, but was open to the public, and was widely appreciated.

To be honest, I really did not want to write about the larger-than-life dynasties, but although small, family controlled companies that still continuously exist. These also have a common factor. Operating under the principle of looking at the long term, not to be influenced by a passing trend, never neglecting to conduct their method of marketing research, which is to watch and absorb what the customer is looking for, the leader of a small family controlled company is required to possess an unsurpassed ability. Due to the length, unfortunately I will end here, to be continued in Part 2.

にも共通点がある。目先にとらわれない長い視点で経営を見ているということともに、マーケット・リサーチ、すなわちカスタマーが何を求めているのか観察するのを怠らないということだ。小さな同族会社のトップこそ、並外れた能力を要求されることにもなる。続きは次話に委ねたい。

ロックフェラー財団の寄付による東京大学附属図書館
築100周年改築工事中(2014年)

第18話

脈々と続く同族会社に学ぶ2
―― 創業者の信念の凄さ

　ご存知の方も多いと思われるが、ドイツのハリボー（Haribo：Hans Riegel Bonn、1920年創業）は、この70年でボン市から世界に販売網を発展させたお菓子屋である。2代目当主のハンス・リーゲル（Hans Riegel：1923～2013年、残念ながら脳腫瘍で最近他界）は、子供はなかったが子供のような無邪気さで1946年以来CEOを務めてきた。その製品は"gummi bears"、海外では"Gold Bears"として名が通っており、"ハリボーは子供たちを幸せにする（Haribo makes children happy）"をキャッチフレーズに生産と従業員を増やし（現在6000人）、工場はボン市本社の周囲から動かず、長年材料を変えずに、高い生産性を維持している。第二次世界大戦では苦難の時を過ごした。収容所に収容されていた弟ポール（Paul）が米軍により開放されたころ、創業者である父が他界した。本人はもとより弟ポールも亡き今後は、ハンスの2人の甥が協調してその意思を継いでいくと思われるが、残された長年のパートナー、アンナ・マリア・ビショップ（Anna Maria Bischop）の幸せと、彼のご冥福を祈って止まない。

　日本で印象に残る同族会社は、岡田屋（現イオン）である。その家訓がなんともユニークである。"大黒柱を動かせ"と聞いている。これは日本離れしており、中国の客家（参照：第1章第17話）にも通ずる発想である。ボンを離れないハリボーとは反対であるが、製造業と小売業の違い

Number Eighteenth

The Survival Capability of Family Controlled Companies (Part 2)
——Relentless Belief of Founders

There may be many of you who are familiar with the German confection manufacturer, Haribo of Bonn, which was established in 1920, and has since that time, for over 70 years were retailing their products globally. The second generation head of the Riegel family, Hans (1923~2013), stricken by a brain tumor, has unfortunately passed away last year. Although Hans himself did not have children, he took the helm of the family business in 1946 and from that time onward, oversaw its operations with the exuberance and passion of a child. One of their products, 'gummi bears', known and recognized outside of Germany, as the 'Golden Bears' was marketed with the phrase "Haribo makes children happy." This product, becoming hugely successful, made way for Haribo to increase their production capacity and employees (currently 6,000). Continuing to operate from their headquarters in the city of Bonn, Haribo has continued, throughout its many years to maintain the original ingredients and sustain a high standard of production.

During the Second World War, the family was not immune to severe hardships and tragedy. Hans' younger brother Paul was confined to a concentration camp, later to be freed by the Americans. Their father, and founder of Haribo, passed away during this period. With the deaths of Hans and Paul, it is Hans' two nephews who will cooperate and manage the family business and maintain the high standards that Haribo is renowned for. I cannot help but wish happiness for Hans' longtime partner, Anna Maria Bischop, and pray that he rests in peace.

There is a family-owned corporation that has particularly made an im-

である。

　また日経新聞の200年企業に出てくる若竹屋酒造所（1999年創業）の家訓は、"若竹屋は先祖より受け継ぎし商いにあらず、子孫より預かりしものなり"という。未来志向の家訓である。私の持論である"終わり良ければすべて良しではなく、終わったことはすべて良し"に通ずるところがあり魅力を感じた。

　この辺で医薬産業を同族会社の視点で覗いてみたい。社名として創業家の名が残っているのは日本も含めて多々あるが、たいていトップにはほぼ同族以外の実力者が就いてその運営に当たっており、パブリック・カンパニーになってしまった。

　しかし、例外が1社ある。独メルク（Merck KGAa）である。いまだに同族で70％の株式を保有している。これも第1章「国際人になるための十戒」第4話で触れたが、3代目当主で米国メルクをニュージャージー州のローウェーに開設したジョージ・メルク（George Merck）の言った"We try never to forget that medicine is for the people. It is not for the profits. The profits follow, and if we have remembered that, they（profits）have never failed to appear..."という家訓をいまだに受け継いでいる。その運営の詳細につき日経新聞の編集委員・大西康之氏による独メルクのインタビュー記事があるので、参照されることをお勧めしたい。

　日本の同族家族は、長子偏重で次男、三男は分家として経営の中枢に入らないケースが多いのではないか。後継者の裾野を広げることも必要なのでは。優秀な婿さんを迎えるのも手段です。スイスのノバルティス社（Novartis）のダニエル・ヴァセエラ（Daniel Vassera：オーナーである

pression on me, and that is Okadaya (the current AEON). Their family motto is especially unique, directly translated, "Move the Major Beam" referring to the major beam supporting a structure. The concept behind this family motto is alien from a Japanese point of view. However, the roots of it may relate to, and be found in the Chinese Hakka (refer to: Ten Commandments in Becoming an Internationally-Minded Person, The Seventeenth Commandment of March 13, 2012) . Opposite, and contrary to Haribo which would not move its operations from the city of Bonn, it is an absolutely vivid example of the difference between manufacturing and retailing.

To add to this, introduced in the Nihon Keizai newspaper's '200 year corporations', is the sake-brewery Wakatakeya, (founded in 1899) and their family motto is "Wakatakeya's business is not handed down from its ancestors, it is kept for its successors." This family motto strongly reflects an emphasis placed on the future. I find this particular motto extremely attractive, and it relates to my personal concept, modifying the often used, "If the end is good, then all is good." I believe that, "Everything with an end is good."

Let's take a look at family-owned corporations within the pharmaceutical industry. Although there are many corporations that still reflect and maintain the founding family name as the corporate's, something seen not only in Japan, but around the world, but the majority of these firms are public companies, managed by extremely efficient corporate managers, who are not from the founding family, but were appointed for their management capabilities.

However, there are, and is an exception. And that is Germany's Merck KGA. The founding family or relations still hold 70% of the company's shares. (Refer to: Ten Commandments in Becoming an Internationally-Minded Person - The Fourth Commandment of April 11, 2011) in which you will find that I have touched upon the 3rd generation leader of the Merck empire, George Merck, who established Merck in the United States, in New Jersey. He has said, "We try never to forget that medicine is for the people. It is not for the profits. The profits follow, and if we have to remember that, they

サンド家の女婿）もしかり。しかし、でき過ぎの声あり。

(profits) have never failed to appear ..." This remains to be the family, or corporate motto to this day. Details of Merck's management can be seen through article written by the Nihon Keizai newspaper's editorial journalist, Mr. Yasuyuki Ohnishi, of an interview he had with Germany's Merck. I suggest that this article be read as reference.

Looking at Japanese family-owned corporations are frequently succeeded by the 'first-born' son, leaving the second and third sons to often establish sub-divisions, or branches of the family, ultimately separated from the center of management of the main company. Perhaps it is necessary to expand the baseline of successors. Accepting a talented and capable bridegroom for the family's daughter is also a method to be considered. A fine example is the case of Switzerland's Novartis, Daniel Vassera, who is married to the owner family, Sand's daughter. It is said,however that he is too good.

第19話

忘れ得ぬ国際人1
──柴﨑正勝氏と「サンデー・サイレンス」

　最近ノーベル化学賞の呼び声高いのは東京大学名誉教授・公益財団法人微生物化学研究所所長兼常務理事である柴﨑正勝氏がその人である。2010年のノーベル化学賞受賞者である根岸英一博士が、弟弟子の如く目をかけてくれているのは嬉しい限りである。畏友・正勝氏との交友は、筆者がオーストラリア国立大学（ANU）から東京大学に戻った1970年、向かいのベンチで実験をしていた修士1年の時にさかのぼる。この辺りの事情は、正勝氏の日経新聞交遊抄（兄の手ほどき）に詳しい。正勝氏がハーバード大学、放射線医学総合研究所、帝京大学、相模中央化学研究所、北海道大学から東京大学へと移りながら、40年余を経ても同じ交流が続いている。夜の11時過ぎにかかる電話は、「ハロー（Hello）」と言うと「ハイ（Hi）」といった具合である。

　その間、正勝氏は日本学士院賞をはじめ、米国化学会、イギリス化学会、スイス化学会などの世界的な賞を総なめにする快進撃を続けている。これは世界がいわゆる"柴﨑化学（Shibasaki Chemistry）"を真に理解・評価したということでもある。

　最近の正勝氏は国際会議において議論をリードし、またディナーを賑やかにするスキルを身に付け、20年前と比べて"ああ、本当に国際人になったなあ"と嬉しくなる。自分と自分の化学に自信があるからできる

Number Nineteenth

Unforgettable International Person(1)
——Prof. Masakatsu Shibasaki and Sunday Silence

High upon recent candidates for the Nobel prize for Chemistry, is Professor Masakatsu Shibasaki, Professor emeritus of the University of Tokyo and Director of the Microbial Chemistry Research Institute. It is with great pleasure that I learn of how Professor Eiichi Negishi, winner of the 2010 Nobel Prize for Chemistry, watches over Prof. Shibasaki as though he would a fellow brother (younger) disciple. My strong friendship and interaction with Masakatsu started in the 70s, when I returned to the University of Tokyo after concluding studies abroad at the Australian National University(ANU). We were in the midst of experimenting on opposite benches, and it was in his first year of the Master's course. More details and information about this period can be found in the article "Respected Friendship (Koyu-sho,Learning from brother) "by Masakatsu, published in the Nihon Keizai newspaper. . Although Masakatsu's academic and research career had taken him from Harvard University, the National Institute of Radiological Science (NIRS), Teikyo University, Sagamihara Central Research Institute , and Hokkaido University, the familiarity and close friendship has always remained strong. The phone calls that ultimately come past 11 at night start off with the English salutations of "Hello" and the response of "Hi".

During this time, Masakatsu has been awarded numerous prestigious recognitions,from The Japan Academy Prize, the American Chemical Society, the Centerary Medal and Lectureship, and the Prelog Award Medal, a phenomenal feat. This is clear evidence that there is a universal understanding and regard among the scientific community toward what is referred to as 'Shi-

柴﨑正勝 東京大学名誉教授と（2011年）

ことである。ただ、人が良すぎるので、時々ハラハラして見ている時もある。

とにかく超多忙で、日本薬学会、そして微化研の将来に向けた改革に取り組んでいるが、目指す仕事の中心はストックホルムである。何もない日曜日は静かにゆっくりしているという"Sunday Silence"の人でもある。正勝氏がストックホルムからの電話に出る時の様子が容易にわかる、私には。これが必然というものである。偶然はない。

Sunday Silenceというと、忘れられない人がもう1人いる。2004年、フロリダから帰るフライトで、隣に大柄のジェントルマンが座った。しばらくすると、「はじめまして……」と言う。それは1989年米国ケンタッキーダービー勝利馬Sunday Silence（サンデーサイレンス）のオーナーであるアーサー・ハンコック氏（Arthur Hancock）だった。筆者は1990年代、サンデーサイレンスに大変興味があり、注目していたこともあって、話がはずんだ。どうしてこのような名前がついたのか聞くと、米国では牧場の子馬（コルト）に名前を推薦してくる慣習があり、このSunday

basaki Chemistry'.

Recently Masakatsu has been leading debates and discussions on the international conference circuit, and at the dinners that follow, has shown his skill at conducting lively and entertaining conversations. In comparison to 20 years ago, I can declare with pleasure that "He has developed into a true international person." This is only obtained when an individual believes in his self, and is confident in his science. However, there are times, due to his trustful and supportive character, in which I watch with not a small amount of nervousness.

Needless to say, Masakatsu is extremely busy. Although he is dedicated and working on the future, and revolutionizing the Pharmaceutical Society of Japan (PSJ), and the Microbial Chemistry Research Center, Microbial Chemistry Research Center, however, the epicenter of his work is Stockholm. On the rare occasions when there is a Sunday in which he can relax, he enjoys a leisurely quite ? Sunday Silence. I can readily perceive how Masakatsu is doing, his condition, when he calls from Stockholm.

When I think of the word of Sunday Silence, there is another unforgettable individual which comes to mind. In 2004, when I was on a flight from Florida returning to Japan, a large gentleman sat next to me. After a while, this gentleman, started to introduce himself. "Hajime-mashite" It turns out that he was Arthur Hancock, the owner of the 1989 Kentucky Derby winner, Sunday Silence.

I myself, in the 90s, was very interested in Sunday Silence, and was paying close attention to this thoroughbred's performance. Thus, the ensuing conversation was that we mutually enjoyed. I inquired on the why the particular name. In response, he explained

Decorated horse in New Year

Silenceは小学生の男子と母親が書いてくれたものなのだそうだ。面白いので採用して、ある子馬にこの名前をつけたという。その子馬が頭角を現し、ケンタッキーダービー馬となり、ライバルのEasy Goer（エーゼー・ゴーアー）を振りきって優勝した。そこで、その男の子を牧場に招いてお祝いをしたらTV局が取材に来て、1時間番組として放映され、大変な人気になったという。これだけで話は終わらない。1990年、オーナーは大きなBusiness decision（事業上の決断）をする。可愛くて手放せなかったのだが、日本の社台ファームの吉田善哉氏の熱意とねばり強い交渉に負けて、種牡馬としてサンデーサイレンスを日本に売却した。その子のディープインパクトは日本ダービー馬を含め3冠馬となり、その孫（ディープインパクトの子）は、今年（2013年）の日本ダービー馬となった。近年の日本馬のドバイやフランス（凱旋門賞）などでの活躍は、このサンデーサイレンスのオーナー氏のビジネス快断のおかげだと思っている。

that in the United States, when there is a new colt, it is customary for potential names to be sent in by the general public. It so happened that this name was sent in by an elementary school boy, and his mother. Feeling that the name was unique, the owner chose Sunday Silence. He named a certain colt with this name. This colt quickly showed its potential, becoming a contester for the Kentucky Derby, leaving behind his rival Easy Goer, and ultimately winning this famed race. The boy who had sent in the name, Sunday Silence was invited to the farm to be part of the winning celebrations, at which a television station was covering the event, making into an hour-long program. After the broadcast of this program, Sunday Silence became extremely popular. The story doesn't end there. In 1990, the owner makes a significant business decision. He was very fond of Sunday Silence, and could not bring himself to let him go, however, through the passionate and persistent negotiations made by Mr. Senya Yoshida representingSyadai Farm in Japan, the owner relented. The sale of Sunday Silence as a stud was finalized. Deep Impact which won the Japan Derby, as well as becoming a Triple Crown winner, was sired by none other than Sunday Silence. The legacy continues with a thoroughbred sired by Deep Impact becoming last year's (2013) Japan Derby contestant. In recent years, Japanese thoroughbreds are showing impressive performances at international races in Dubai and France's famous Prix de l'Arc de Triomphe, and I think that it is perhaps through Mr. Hancock's business decision that this was made possible.

第20話

忘れ得ぬ国際人2
―― C. ロビン・ガネリン氏の「ヒスタミン・ロマンス」

　米国において発売(1978年)と同時に十二指腸潰瘍の手術が激減したという革命的医薬品シメチジン/タガメット (Cimetidine/Tagamet®) の発明者であるロンドン大学 (UCL：University College London) の名誉教授であるC.ロビン・ガネリン氏(Charon Robin Ganellin)がその人である。

　彼との交誼は、1991年ガネリン氏が国際純正応用化学連合 (IUPAC、オックスフォード) の医薬品化学(medicinal chemistry)の委員会委員長兼幹事役 (Titular member) にイギリス化学会を代表して就任した時からだ。もう20年余りに及ぶ。ちなみに筆者は、1974年から1981年まで日本学術会議を代表して幹事役(Titular)を務めていた。

　ガネリン氏はまさに誠心誠意の方で、よく他人(ヒト)の話を聞き、1つ1つ糸を解してまとめ上げ、強いリーダーシップを発揮する人である。優れた科学者・化学者であると同時に、どのようにしてこのような人格を身につけたのであろうか。それには師でもあるノーベル生理・医学賞受賞者であるジェームズ・ブラック卿 (Dr. Sir James Black) を抜きには語れない。

　最近のガネリン氏の "Sir James Black and the Discovery of Cimetidine" と題する講演を眺めてみたい。御高承のとおり、ブラック卿は高血圧症

Number Twentieth
Unforgettable International Person(2)
——Prof. Robin Ganellin and Histamine Romance

In the United States, with the introduction in 1978, of a revolutionary drug, Cimetidine/Tagamet®, surgical procedures in duodenal ulcers dramatically decreased. The drug was discovered through the medicinal chemistry analysis of Dr C. Robin Ganellin, now Emeritus Professor at University College London, working together with Sir James Black.

I had the great honor of making his acquaintance in 1991 when, as a representative of England's chemistry society, he was the Section Chair and Titular Member of the Committee of Medicinal Chemistry Section of the International Union of Pure Applied Chemistry/IUPAC (Oxford), and this relationship has continued for over 20 years. I, myself, have served as the Titular of the Science Council of Japan from 1974 until 1981.

Prof. Ganellin is an extremely sincere man, who is known for intently listening to what an individual has to say. He possesses a unique method of unraveling any issue or problem, thread by thread, to bring the elements together to introduce a solution, in which he reflected his strong leadership. In addition to being brilliant scientist, as well as, chemist, I often wondered how his personality had developed. To further understand Prof. Ganellin, reference must be made to his mentor, Dr. Sir James Black, Nobel Laureate of Physiology or Medicine in 1988.

Recently Prof. Ganellin has lectured on "Sir James Black and the Discovery of Cimetidine".As many of you are aware, Dr. Sir James Black is an accomplished and great scientist, who discovered and developed TWO (2) "First in Class" medicines, such as: a beta-Blocker (Propranolol®) as an anti-hyperten-

薬β-ブロッカー（プロプラノール®）ならびに胃酸分泌抑制剤であるシメチジン（前述）を生体メカニズムから理論的に発見・開発した偉人である。約100余年前、1901年日本人の高峰譲吉・上中啓三により結晶化されたアドレナリンより強い作用の誘導体を、後年（1950年代）探していたグループ（ICI）に対し、ブラック卿はその副作用に注目してアドレナリン受容体（β）の抑制剤を発見・開発することにより抗高血薬ができると予測した。そして見事にβ-ブロッカーとしてプロプラノールを発見し、開発に成功したのである。

その後この考えを胃酸分泌を促すヒスタミンの受容体（H2）に応用し、H2受容体をブロックすることによって胃酸分泌を抑え、十二指腸潰瘍の治療ができるのではないかと予測した。そのためブラック卿は招かれてSK&Fに赴任して、ヒスタミンH2リセプターの抑制剤の発見を目指した。このシメチジンの発見と開発は、ガネリン氏なしに語れないのも事実である。時に1964年、SK&Fの化学部長であったガネリン氏（のちに取締役）との出会いとなる。ガネリン氏は、H2-プロジェクトの責任者となり、ヒスタミンH1リセプターに作用なく、H2リセプターを抑制し、胃酸分泌を抑える化学物質の探索を、薬理作用検定（2種類）と併せて強力に進めた。そして1978年のシメチジン（商品名タガメット）の開発に到るまでの13年に及ぶ壮絶な戦いが始まったのである。4年間で200化合物を合成したが、目指す作用は得られず、SK&F米国本社からプロジェクト中止の指令があったが、それを無視し続行する。ここは、ジェームス卿の力だろうか。H2のアンタゴニストを発見し、見事に胃酸分泌を抑え、28日以内で12指張潰瘍が完治した！　患者700人のうち7人に顆粒球減少症が見つかり開発中止。構造変換によりシメチジンにたどり着くまで13年を費やした。ここで非常に興味があるのは、ジェームス卿は医師でありながら、開発化合物が決まるとその場を離れ

sive and cimetidine (Tagamet®) as an H2-blocker of gastric-acid secretion. Roughly 100 years ago, in 1901, two Japanese chemists researching in the United States, JokichiTakamine and Keizo Uenaka, developed crystalized Adrenaline. Years later (in the 1950s) a group of researchers (ICI) were searching for a higher-potency derivative as acardiotonic, in the meantime, Sir James Black went on to discover pronethalola blocker of Adrenaline receptor(β), as well as predicting that this would become an anti-hypertensive medicine. From this, ICI developed the anti-hypertensive medicine, Inderal®. Through utilizing the same method, Dr.Black, recognizing that histamine was stimulating acid secretion, predicted the potential of treating duodenal ulcers by using a histamine H_2-blocker although the histamine H_2 receptor was still unknown. These series of breakthroughs ultimately led to the invitation by SK&F (in England) to Dr Black, who joined the firm and continued his search for a suppressant of the putative histamine H_2-receptor. The road to the discovery and development of Cimetidine would not have been possible without Dr. Ganellin. The year was 1964, the two met at SK&F where Dr. Ganellin was head of medicinal chemistry (later becoming a board member).

Dr. Ganellin became responsible forthe chemistry of the H_2 project. Facing the results that histamine H_1 receptor had no impact, he vigorously sought chemicals that would block the histamine H_2-receptor acting on gastric-acid secretion while assessing thepharmacological effect from screening (2 types). It was the beginning of a 13-year grueling battle to development and, in 1976, Cimetidine (product name, Tagamet?) was ready for application for a license for treatment. In the first 4 years, after200 chemical compounds had been screened without reaching the desired effect, SK&F U.S. headquarters ordered the project to be terminated;ignoring this order, research in England continued onward. Discovering anH_2 antagonist, thatwas brilliantly effective toward suppressing gastric-acid secretion, resulted in the complete recovery from a duodenal ulcer within 28 days. Of the 700 patients treated, 7 developed granulocytopenia, and so development was terminated. Altering the chemical structure, then led to Cimetidine.It had taken 13 years overall. It is

てしまうことだ。それは、企業のプロの仕事だという。プロプラノールの時（ICI）と同様、1973年にロンドン大学の教授に転出している。

　さて、ここで"A Histamine Romance"に触れなくてはならない。フランスのパリにある国立健康・医学研究所（Institute of Health and Medical Research）のシュヴァルツ教授が、SK&Fの論文を見て、最初の胃酸分泌抑制作用のある化合物であったブルマミド（burimamide）のサンプルを依頼してきた。それを提供したFK&FとINSERMとの間に研究提携ができて、交流が始まった。1986年ガネリン氏はジェームス卿と同様UCLに戻ったが、INSERMにいたのが、脳内ヒスタミンとH3受容体の働きを研究していたのがガネリン氏の現在のベターハーフであるモニーク（Monique Garbarg）である。皆に祝福されて、脳腫瘍で妻を亡くした（1997年）ガネリン氏と久しく独身だったモニークがめでたく結ばれた（2003年）というまさに"ヒタミン・ロマンス"である。二人には、何回か会っているが、エジプトのカイロが印象に残っている。

C. ロビン・ガネリン ロンドン大学名誉教授と妻モニーク

here that a vital philosophy is shared. Although Sir James Black was a physician, after a to-be-developed chemical compound was established, he leaves the research environment. It is said that he said "It is now up to the business professionals." Similar to when he discovered Pronethalol (ICI).In1973, Black returned to teaching and went to University College London (UCL).

It is here that I think it is necessary to touch upon "A Histamine Romance". The setting is Paris, France. Prof. Schwartz of the Institute of Health and Medical Research (INSERM), upon reading a SK&F paper, requested a sample of the first gastric-acid secretion blocker chemical compound burimamide. Responding to this request became the beginning of a research alliance and interaction between SK&F and INSERM. In 1986, Ganellinwentto UCL as Prof of Medicinal Chemistry. His better-half, Dr Monique Garbarg was researching the effects that theH3 receptor has upon histamine within the brain at INSERM. Prof. Ganellin, who was then single, having lost his wife to a brain tumor in 1997, met Monique and the two were married in 2003, "A Histamine Romance". I have had the pleasure of meeting the two on several occasions, however, meeting with them at the IUPAC Conference in Egypt's Cairo, has left a lasting impression.

あとがき

　本書の出版をお奨めいただいた㈱日本医療企画社長・林諄様に感謝申し上げます。

　また高校、大学、大学院時代、三菱時代、アップジョン時代、E・リリー時代、米国研究製薬工業協会時代、そして現東京大学薬友会時代に御指導いただいた方々、特に故 山田俊一東京大学名誉教授、故A・アルバート名誉教授(オーストラリア国立大学)、小宮山宏前東京大学総長・東京大学名誉教授、W・L・F・アルマレゴ名誉フェロー（オーストラリア国立大学）、柴﨑正勝東京大学名誉教授、寺田弘徳島大学名誉教授、米川耕一弁護士夫妻、故T・クーパー（アップジョン）、ノーム・マーシャル夫妻(アップジョン)、シドニー・トーレル(E・リリー)、ジョン・レックライター（E・リリー）、R・ガネリン ロンドン大学名誉教授、U・タグリーバー（メルク）、H・クック（前米国商務省）、花輪弘之(米国大使館／日本)、R・ファイク（ワイス）、T・ガンブルトン（アップジョン）、そして近藤達也理事長（PMDA）、二川一男官房長（厚生労働省）、藤原康弘局長(国立がん研究センター)、G・ヴァン-ボッケレン(アサーシス)の皆様に御礼を申し上げます。

　その間、仕事の支えをいただいた秘書(A.Administrator)の方々：佐川久美子、橋本恵子、串田万里子、千葉恵、松久ヨシ子、杉本美嘉子、宇佐見浩子、九里由紀美、日高昌子、佐藤麻衣子、和田瑠璃子、柴田侑子、坂本朋子の皆様に、特に富永広三氏(アップジョン)に感謝いたします。

Acknowledgements

Toshihiko Kobayashi

I would like to express my gratitude to Mr. Jun Hayashi, President of K.K. Nihon Iryo Kikaku for encouraging me to write this book.

To my many friends and fellow classmates during my high school, university and graduate school days, the wonderful colleagues and senior management during my days with Mitsubishi Petrochemical, Upjohn, Eli Lilly, the Pharmaceutical Research and Manufacturers of America (PhRMA), and to the learned members of the University of Tokyo Akamon Gakuyu Kai from whom I currently continue to receive invaluable advice and guidance. Unmeasurable gratitude to the late Professor Emeritus Shunichi Yamada, University of Tokyo, the late Professor Emeritus Adrian Albert ,Australian National University(ANU), W.L.F. Armarego, Honorary Fellow, (ANU), Former President of University of Tokyo and Professor Emeritua Hiroshi Komiyama ,Professor Emeritus Masakatsu Shibasaki, University of Tokyo,Professor Emeritus Hiroshi Terada (Tokushima) ,the late T. Cooper (Upjohn) Dr and Mrs. Norm Marshall (Upjohn), Sydney Taurel (Eli Lilly and Company), John Lechleiter (Eli Lilly and Company) , Professor Emeritus R. Ganellin, University of London, U. Tagliever (Merck), H. Cook (former U.S. Department of Commerce), Hiroyuki Hanawa (U.S. Embassy, Japan), R. Fike (Wyeth),T.Gambleton , (Upjohn and Pfizer)), and Director General Tatsuya Kondo (PMDA), Deputy Vice Minister Kazuo Futagawa (MHLW), Director Yasuhiro Fujiwara (National Cancer Research Center), G. van Bokkelen (Athersys).

I would like to thank the following secretaries and administrators who have provided me with invaluable support;; Kumiko Sagawa, Keiko Hashimoto, Mariko Kushida, Megumi Chiba, Yoshiko Matsuhisa, Mikako Sugi-

本書のイラストを担当いただいた三宅留美氏に感謝いたします。また本書に掲載した全41話を連載いただいた国際商業出版（株）の編集長岩垂広、編集委員上野蘭子の両氏に感謝いたします。また本書の編集を担当された（株）日本医療企画の松村藤樹、吉見知浩、能登谷勇の皆様、種々お手伝いいただいた薬学振興会の吉川将史氏、CCCコンサルタントの後藤忠良、シェリー藤沼の両氏にあわせて感謝いたします。

　本書を、昨年（2013年）天に召されましたが48年にわたり支えてくれた妻順子（1965～2013年）、いまだ惜別の心止まぬ早世の次女陽子（1991年）に捧げ、ありがとうと申し上げたい。また長男一彦一家（5人）と長女夏子の大嶋家（4人）の発展を、この場を借りて、祈りたく存じます。

小林利彦

moto, Hiroko Usami, Yukimii Kuri , Masako Hidaka, Maiko Sato, Ruriko Wada, Yuko Shibata, and Tomoko Sakamoto, and especially Kozo Tominaga(Upjohn).

Thanks to Rumi Miyake who was responsible for the wonderful illustrations with Rumi-mark. I am grateful to Editor-in-Chief Hiroshi Iwadare and Editor Ranko Ueno of Kokusai Shogyo Publishing (K.K.) for publishing a series of 41 installments of this book. This book would not have been possible without the expertise of Fujiki Matsumura, Tomohiro Yoshimi, and Isamu Notoya of (K.K.) Nihon Iryo Kikaku who were responsible for the editing of the 41 stories. I wish to express my gratitude to Masafumi Yoshikawa of Yakugaku Shinkokai, who has provided countless assistance, as well as Tadayoshi Goto and Sherrie Fujinuma of CC Consultants (English).

I dedicate this book to my wife, Junko who was called to heaven last year (2013), after 48 years (1965–2013) of the consistent support and care she gave me, and to Yoko, our second daughter, who left this world so young (1991), will always remain special in my heart. I want say, Thank you so much . I pray that my son, Kazuhiko and his family of five, along with my daughter Natsuko and her family of four, the Ohshima's, will enjoy all the pleasures and joy life has to give.

● 著者略歴

小林 利彦（こばやし・としひこ）

東京大学（薬）卒業（1961年）。オーストラリア国立大学大学院（博士：医化学、1970年）。三菱時代（1971〜1985年）、米国製薬トップ10会社（アップジョン社・E．リリー社）時代（1986〜2001年）、米国研究製薬工業協会（PhRMAワシントンDC）時代（2001〜2012年）、そして国際純正応用化学連合（英オックスフォード、1973年〜現在）、アジア医薬化学連合（1992年〜現在）を通して国内外の人脈にいつも助けられ心より深謝。
現在、東京大学赤門学友会顧問、東京大学薬友会会長、米国シリコンバレー バイオベンチャーの顧問など。

国際人になるためのInsight Track
──モーゼの十戒に学べ 【英訳文付】

2014年7月20日 第1版第1刷発行

著 者	小林 利彦
発 行 者	林 諄
発 行 所	株式会社日本医療企画
	〒101-0033 東京都千代田区神田岩本町4-14
	神田平成ビル
	TEL 03-3256-2861（代表）
	FAX 03-3256-2865
	http://www.jmp.co.jp
印 刷 所	大日本印刷株式会社

ISBN978-4-86439-293-8 C0036
ⓒToshihiko Kobayashi 2014, Printed in Japan

定価はカバーに表示しています。
本書の全部または一部の複写・複製・転訳等を禁じます。これらの許諾については小社までご照会ください。